Architecture Connecting: Living Structures

Louisiana Museum of Modern Art & Lars Müller Publishers

Content

Architecture Connecting is a new exhibition series at Louisiana Museum of Modern Art that explores the relationship between architecture and society's social, cultural and technological spheres – more specifically, architecture's relationship to the natural sciences, to biology. Under the title *Living Structures,* three invited architectural studios have very different takes on science, but share a focus on biology. Italy's ecoLogicStudio, based in London, works with biodigital architecture, in which living organisms – for example, walls of algae that can purify the air – form part of the architecture; Atelier LUMA from Arles in the south of France embraces bioregionality, creating new materials from natural resources in the local area, such as sunflower seeds and salt; and American Jenny Sabin focusses on bioresponsive architecture, researching everything from flowers to chicken hearts on a cellular level before upscaling it.

Despite its name, the Louisiana Museum of Modern Art has a long tradition of showing architecture exhibitions. Architecture, unlike art, serves society in a more direct way, and the former is thus radically different from the latter, although architecture does also contribute aesthetic experience to our lives. Architects are always already working at the intersection of sciences, but are able to ori-

ent themselves in different ways, with greater emphasis on one science over another. Is architecture first and foremost about construction and material, a science-based practice that works with factual conditions such as gravity? Is it conceived with a prevailing focus on its social power? Or is it conceived as an aesthetic statement, with the technical aspects of its construction merely acting as midwife? Architecture is a practice where the boundaries between philosophies and orientations are fluid. It is naturally dependent on and bound by physics, but again worthless without a sense of the humanistic and aesthetic project. Synthesis is the desirable scenario for creation.

In the presence of major questions over the climate, this synthesis only becomes more important, and the branches of knowledge to which the architect must relate more numerous. In order to be built, architecture has always had connections to a number of fields of knowledge, but those connections exist more and more in its conception, in the way spaces are imagined in the first place. This exhibition and those to come in the series explore architecture's connections to other sciences, how some connections are more apparent today, and how these connections are responses to current social issues, thus altering the practice of architecture.

Most recently, we presented the exhibition series *The Architect's Studio,* where visitors to the museum were able to peek into the engine rooms of a number of younger architects. In that exhibition series we moved further and further away from the typical concept of architecture where the building is the work, and this exhibition series is a natural extension of that. The three guest studios in the new *Architecture Connecting* series do not (yet) build large buildings, and are perhaps not typical architects in that sense. They do, however, experiment with alternative ways of understanding and thinking about architecture, and are, in a way, renegotiating the role of the 'typical architect' – the architects of the future may operate within these connections rather than just in the work itself.

This catalogue, designed by graphic designer Anni's, is organized in the spirit of the exhibition: nature has been taken into consideration both in terms of selecting paper that is either recycled or made from materials other than wood – one of the papers is made from a byproduct of sugar cane production – and in terms of ensuring that as little paper as possible is wasted. Similarly, parts of the exhibition are built with as much material recycled from the museum's previous exhibitions as possible, and with pre-existing structures such as scaffolding that can be returned and reused by others.

Thanks

We would like to thank everyone involved in the production of the exhibition and catalogue. First, to the three guest studios: ecoLogicStudio, Claudia Pasquero and Marco Poletto; Atelier LUMA and artistic director Jan Boelen; and Jenny Sabin, JSStudio and JSLab. Thank you so much for your commitment and willingness to create distinct works and projects for this particular exhibition. Thank you to all the staff at the three studios who have made this possible. We would also like to thank architect Tobias Øhrstrøm and sustainable design engineer Kirsten Lynge from Søuld, architect and PhD Line Kjær Frederiksen, and professor and architect Anne Beim/CINARK, Royal Danish Academy – Architecture, Design, Conservation in Copenhagen, thatcher Thomas Gerner, interim design director Christian Andersen and product development engineer Torben Jensen from Fritz Hansen, artist Sara Martinsen, The Seed Station/Naturstyrelsen, and Torben L. Riis from Nordic Sugar A/S.

Special thanks to the interlocutors for this catalogue's conversations with the three studios, Mette Ramsgaard Thomsen, Mario Carpo and Harshim Sarkis. Thanks also to Mette Ramsgaard Thomsen for sparring and reviewing Jenny Sabin's texts in Danish translation.

Finally we extend our gratitude to Realdania for the continuos and focused support of the Louisiana's engagement in architecture.

Poul Erik Tøjner
Director, Louisiana Museum of Modern Art

Mette Marie Kallehauge
Curator

Kjeld Kjeldsen
Curator

The exhibition *Architecture Connecting: Living Structures* explores the relationship between architecture and natural science, specifically highlighting the presence of biology in architecture today. Biology is the science of living organisms and their interactions with the environment. How do architects incorporate insights from the living world in their work?

We have invited three architecture studios with different approaches to transdisciplinary practice: ecoLogicStudio, Atelier LUMA and Jenny Sabin Studio. All three work with research on biological life as an integrated part of their aesthetic practice. At the same time as creating new materials and new architecture, their work is as much a negotiation of the methods and field of architecture. ecoLogicStudio explores nature's affinity with the digital sphere at the cross-section of algorithms and algae in an attempt to integrate natural processes such as photosynthesis in architecture. Atelier LUMA applies bioregional tools and site-specific production, transforming raw materials into designs rooted in local knowledge. And Jenny Sabin's focus is learning from cellular processes and transferring these natural mechanisms to architecture. Together these studios show the scope of transdisciplinary architectural practices that engage with other forms of knowledge and science and treat nature as a collaborative partner. Each of their projects represent hopeful and innovative responses to the biodiversity crisis.

Tentacular Thinking

Architecture needs to involve other fields of research to justify building in what has been called the 'Anthropocene' – a concept that has been in focus in architecture exhibitions at Louisiana Museum of Modern Art in recent years.[1] Despite some criticism, especially in an era where humankind and the climate are inseparable, the concept of the Anthropocene has resonated across the globe. During the past millennia of industrialisation and technological innovation in the Western world we apparently lost sight of the fact that humans are not separate from nature but *are* nature. Even though the Anthropocene is not officially recognized as a geological epoch, the concept has been embraced by a wide range of researchers in different fields. Due to the vast amount of CO_2 emissions produced by the building industry architects have no choice but to address the biodiversity crisis. The widespread interest in characterizing our age on the basis of the relationship between humankind and geology reflects the scale of the climate and biodiversity crisis. It also highlights the growing collaboration between different fields of expertise and the erasure of boundaries between those who can contribute to dealing with a crisis we all face.

It is precisely this dissolution of boundaries between different professions that is in focus in the exhibition. The Anthropocene is interesting in itself, but it is the criticism and renegotiation of the concept that points in the direction of a transdisciplinary practice.[2] The Anthropocene has been critiqued for the anthropocentrism at the root of the word and concept: for conceiving of nature and humans as separate and neglecting other forces, like those of nature, that impact on the relationship between the planet and humankind. American biologist and philosopher Donna Haraway has entered

Mette Marie Kallehauge

debates on the Anthropocene with the concept of 'the Chthulucene', a neologism probably rooted in the name of the spider *Pimoa Cthulhu* worshipped in animistic cultures as a goddess of the earth. For Haraway none of the terms used to describe our age – the Capitalocene, the Plantationocene, the Anthropocene, etc. – break with human hegemony. The Chthulucene is her attempt to present a concept with a narrative of our shared history across species and everything that demands what she calls 'tentacular' thinking – thinking *with* and not *about* the earth.[3]

It is this more 'tentacular' thinking that becomes manifest when the architects and designers in this catalogue describe methods of working that are in close dialogue with nature and natural science. Humans are not the only thinking species, nature too has many different forms of intelligence. We know that other animals have language despite not knowing what they are saying. We also know that fungi form networks that 'collaborate'. The idea is that we have to try to understand and work with them, these potentially more intelligent beings in nature: the trees, the algae, the fungi. Taking a closer look at the relationship between architecture and natural science springs from the realization that architecture too must go beyond the Anthropocene: that architecture could be nature too. Where does this understanding begin? A simple approach is to expand the boundaries of architecture through connections with other fields of knowledge and science: a transdisciplinary architectural practice.

Transdisciplinarity in Practice

The concept of the Anthropocene emerged in response to climate change and the role of humankind in driving it, laying the foundations for a different kind of transdisciplinary research that merges quantifiable sciences with less measurable forms of knowledge. Fields like geology, biology, mythology and art start to translate each other's languages. Anna Lowenhaupt Tsing is one of the world's leading anthropologists and has spent many years researching the Anthropocene, also at the research institute AURA – Aarhus University Research on the Anthropocene – where the methods from anthropology, biology and philosophy meet to create new images and new ways of understanding the age we live in. On transdisciplinary research she says:

"It's actually an extremely important part of our conception. Our goal is to argue that the place to begin with these necessary transdisciplinary collaborations is in engagement with the details of the world rather than working out philosophy first and then trying to hammer it down into the world. We need to begin instead with ants or with lichens or with other ways of knowing the world – snake spirits and volcanoes – and to build out from them a sense of what is possible in terms of bringing scientists and humanists together and in making an intervention into the terrible hegemony of business as usual."[4]

Tsing describes a methodology that unites scientists and humanists who begin by collaboratively identifying a research subject and developing shared methods. It is about understanding one's own field by taking untraditional paths – using methods from other fields or simply attempting to understand other living beings. Can we learn to study other species and in doing so rethink architectural practices? Or as Ting says, not only study other living organisms but act on their terms.[5] This is what art does: it engages with all the substructures and superstructures of our lives and that for which there may be no scientific evidence – at least according to conventional Western research practices. To engage meaningfully with the Anthropocene, evidence-based research must grapple with these elements and embrace Haraway's 'tentacular thinking'.

When Tsing talks about snake spirits and lichen, it is about cultivating a consciousness and sensitivity to that which lies beyond what we have been taught, beyond what researchers in science and the humanities acquire through formal education. ecoLogicStudio likewise points to architecture not only being about finding new technologies but also cultivating new sensibilities – new ways of sensing and perceiving. Here architects find themselves in an interesting position at the intersection of scientific and humanistic approaches. They create solutions in the real world using tangible materials to make buildings that contend with forces like gravity, traction and pressure. Simultaneously they draw from the humanities, where analysis is based on less quantifiable values such as people's well-being and sense of space, movement and aesthetic qualities. Research that is genuinely transdisciplinary does not merely take two complete ways of thinking and glue them together in a joint statement, something we explore in this, the first exhibition in the series.

The logics of nature and biology become clear when the architect zooms in on living organisms under the microscope, organisms that were on earth millions of years before us and will probably be here long after. What makes such organisms robust? What makes them able to grow, coordinate and survive? And what can we learn from their 'knowledge'? We invite algae, mould, fungi, salt crystals and the flowering plant *Arabidopsis* (thale cress) inside the museum because we recognize their patterns, and because they can 'think like us' – or perhaps we have learnt how to think from them? In the exhibition the codes behind forms of nature and life are investigated to show the obvious qualities of nature as a planner, designer and source of inspiration for new materials.

Bio-Digitality – ecoLogicStudio

Claudia Pasquero and Mario Poletto, the founders of ecoLogicStudio, describe themselves as practice-based researchers who focus on changing the methods of the architect. The subject of their research is non-human living organisms, a focus catalysed during their individual PhD research and through teaching at institutes such as the Synthetic Landscape Lab at the University of Innsbruck and the Urban Morphogenesis Lab at Bartlett School of Architecture in London. They introduce these living organisms into architecture and urban planning, for example by physically integrating algae and thereby photosynthesis into the built environment. Likewise, they collaborate with living organisms in urban planning, learning from their 'thinking' and thereby challenging established norms in society and urban life by investigating the benefits of the 'knowledge' of bacteria, algae, fungi and spiders – their ability to organise, survive and create new life.

Inviting these organisms into the process and allowing them to set the parameters for the digital tools used by architects creates the opportunity to rethink the nature of architecture and the conditions of life in modern buildings and cities. This enables us to regard such organisms as part of cities and architecture instead of something to be hidden away and avoided. Bacteria have not been popular in the development of modern cities based on sanitation and the separation of people and waste. This development might have increased our standard of living, improved our health and made our lives longer, but bacteria are diverse, and we now know that many of them are vital to human life. ecoLogicStudio challenge our conventional perceptions of nature – typically thought of as a serene forest lake or a stunning landscape – by including microscopic nature that is equally essential.

Nature in cities is not limited to parks and gardens. For the exhibition at Louisiana Museum of Modern Art ecoLogicStudio have wedded the 'thinking' of living organisms and digital tools they call 'bio-digitality' to create the installation *Deep Forest*.[6] The forest brings together different elements of the studio's work, including the incorporation of photosynthesis in architecture. Based on a satellite and topological map of Humlebæk where the museum is located an algorithm based on a slime mould, an intelligent organism capable of finding the most favourable path between sources of nourishment, has been used to create a landscape of points where the studio has inserted 'tree trunks' to create a bio-digital forest or cyber garden. The forest is comprised of 20 biodegraders – 3D printed birch tress filled with coffee ground that has developed mycelium fungus to create biodegradable tree trunks – 46 algae reactors with bubbling, growing algae in over-sized test tubes that clean the air and absorb CO_2, and 100 repurposed birch trunks from forest clearing in the Danish region of Zealand. *Deep Forest* presents a scenario for a possible future in which nature has to be created by humans at the same time as providing insight into essential elements of ecoLogicStudio's research.

Bio-Regionalism – Atelier LUMA

In Arles, France, Atelier LUMA's research design lab develops new building materials and designs based on the nature of the local region. The people working in the labs include architects, designers, engineers and biologists who constantly develop new design strategies, mapping tools and production chains according to the mantra that materials are heavy and should therefore be located on the site, whereas people and ideas are light and can travel.[7] Their methodology is based on four pillars: finding new materials and people in the given bioregion; connecting with local companies and stakeholders; engaging new knowledge about the region, unutilised materials and new production methods in the pre-existing infrastructure, and sharing the knowledge produced so related materials, production methods and companies elsewhere in the world can benefit from the studio's know-how and tools.[8]

Atelier LUMA's work cannot be reduced to critical regionalism. It is what could be termed *bio-genius loci*, in which the spirit of place is not only about experienced and sensed spatial qualities and a sensitivity to traditional building materials and techniques but resides in the entire ecosystem and production process. Every parameter constitutes 'the place': nature, biology, history, culture, traditional crafts and unutilised materials, but also local companies, the social infrastructure and possible upscaling for future industrial production. Atelier LUMA insists that the work it does is relevant to the age we live in. Sustainability terms that are often reduced to slogans are taken seriously at the lab in Arles. Take the recycling of plastic in the so-called 'circular economy'. Why recycle a material that is of poor quality to begin with and deteriorates more and more as it is recycled before finally being incinerated? Why not find an entirely biodegradable material to replace it?

The work of Atelier LUMA is appealingly beautiful, honest and simple in design. But the designs are not the result of simply stripping them of anything unnecessary – theirs is not a form of aesthetic minimalism aimed at reducing energy consumption. Instead they are driven by the tireless aspiration to enrich people's lives with architecture and design of high aesthetic value. People still get ideas and create things, a basic human instinct that should be made visible. In Arles they stand in the mud and sea in their wellingtons, harvest sunflowers, and print, form and fire bricks out of natural materials we have never even imagined using. For the exhibition at Louisiana Atelier LUMA's fieldwork in the local area of Humlebæk has resulted in several bioregional materials. They have developed a special 3D printed Humlebæk brick, made largely out of paper and cardboard waste from Louisiana and coloured using dyes from plants in the nature surrounding the museum. Similarly, they have worked on developing an alternative method for producing typical Danish plug sockets, replacing the standard ABS plastic with a bioplastic made from surplus molasses sourced from sugar factories in Zealand. This bioplastic is transformed into a leather-like material that can be assembled using thermo-compression. The bioregional project that falls under the 'connecting' category consists of a collaboration with the furniture manufacturer Fritz Hansen to produce Arne Jacobsen's classical 7 chair in veneer made from the invasive tree of heaven that grows in both Denmark and Arles. Atelier LUMA have produced a limited amount of veneer that Fritz Hansen have used to produce a small number of chairs. The results are not perfect according to the standards of the company, but they are a step towards bringing more sustainable types of wood into the manufacture of furniture. For Atelier LUMA the chairs also represent an opportunity to celebrate the imperfection of invasive and overlooked species of tree as part of a new design paradigm.

Bioresponsive Architecture – Jenny Sabin Studio
Jenny Sabin Studio in the USA is the third architect we have invited to participate in the exhibition. Her work is deeply rooted in the research environment at Cornell University in Ithaca, New York. Indeed all her projects are part of a research project. In the exhibition they are presented through five overarching fields of research: Morphogenesis and Multicellular Systems, Digital Ceramics and Additive Manufacturing, Responsive Textile Materials, Folding Material Effects, and Structural Color and Designing with Light. All five fields have emerged out of a strong interest in understanding the adaptability of nature and the possibility of transferring some of its intelligent mechanisms to materials such as bricks, glass and textiles, as well as inventing new, as yet unknown materials. Sabin's fascination with nature can be seen in the light of the rising need for architecture that can withstand climate change but is also motivated by an interest in people's interaction with the materials to create optimal conditions for social life and bring qualities like light into architecture in ways that respond to its surroundings. Sabin studied under the engineer Cecil Balmond, who exhibited in Louisiana's architecture series *Frontiers of Architecture* in 2007.[9] In the exhibition he opened the door between mathematics and architecture, exploring the way the hidden order of nature always lies behind the forms we surround ourselves with. Starting with Balmond's pioneering engineering work, Sabin has taken mathematics, algorithms and biological research a step further and on a much smaller scale, i.e. at cell level. Here everything from chicken hearts and flowers to cancer cells can be investigated to see and understand the patterns Sabin and the research unit she is part of call "Understanding the Rules of Life".[10] The research is aimed at identifying what we can learn from nature's designs in order to create architecture that behaves like a living organism. For Sabin the first stage is creating tools that can convert the knowledge she gathers in collaboration with experts in fields like biology. The design processes are then converted from nature into small-scale prototypes, for example Polybrick II, a brick inspired by bones that has a stronger and more adaptive structure and can therefore

11

be assembled instead of using mortar. The next step is up-scaling the prototype to create a potential building ecol-ogy, although so far this has been limited to large spatial installations used to test light-absorbing and light-emit-ting textiles and structural colours, i.e. colours that do not use pigment but deploy the connection between the structure of the material and soundwaves we can per-ceive. Based on her love of algorithms, Sabin has col-laborated with Microsoft on an installation that changes form and colour via facial recognition and reading the mood of staff in the company's building where the work is installed.

Sabin's work embodies the encounter between compu-tational power and living organisms. The layout of Sabin's contribution to the exhibition is based on a cellular au-tomata algorithm fed with information on the frequency and flow of visitors, the possibilities and limitations of the space, and the size of the exhibited objects and their re-lationship to Sabin's five fields of research. In simplified terms, the algorithm is based on a grid. Each cell in the grid changes in relationship to changes in its neighbour cell in a feedback loop. The gallery thereby has the same properties as those we see in a dynamic biological space like those in Sabin's research.

Working with the three studios makes it clear that ar-chitecture is taking paths that generate a new kind of transdisciplinarity in architecture. The incorporation of nature and biology is not based on any romantic idea about abolishing industry, digital tools and robots, but on linking the intelligent tools humans have created with a contemporary view of nature. The three studios in the exhibition can appear semi-dogmatic in their approach-es to design, but on closer examination maybe they just have a more realistic way of viewing the world. When they zoom in on the scale of algae, salt crystals and chicken

hearts they underline the need to establish a new form of sensory perception – and an entirely new form of ge-ometry to be taught at schools of architecture worldwide in order to build the foundations of the architecture of the future.

1 Particularly the last of the six exhibitions in our series *The Architect's Studio* with Kenyan Cave_bureau, addresses the concept of the Anthropocene. Cave_bureau's main project was 'The Anthropocene Museum' and took a critical stance on the exclusion of the Global South implicit to the concept but also the representation of climate challenges and their solutions. Earlier exhibitions with Elemental (2018), Anupama Kundoo (2020) and Forensic Architecture (2022) also addressed issues central to the Anthropocene. These include climate change but also social and humanitarian crises. Mette Marie Kallehauge, Kabage Karanja et al., *The Architect's Studio: Cave_bureau,* Louisiana Museum of Modern Art, 2023.
2 Nils Bubandt, *Seks teser om Antropocæn* in the online journal *Turbulens: Forum for samtidsrefleksion*, https://turbulens.net/, 2018.
3 Donna Haraway, *Staying with the Trouble: Making Kin in the Chthulucene*, Duke University Press, 2016.
4 https://edgeeffects.net/anna-tsing/
5 See, for example, the website *Feral Atlas* curated and edited by Anna L. Tsing, Jennifer Deger, Alder Keleman Saxena and Feifei Zhou, feralatlas.org
6 Read more about bio-digitality in the conversation between ecoLogicStudio and Mario Carpo in this catalogue, pp. 12-21. See also Claudio Pasquero and Marco Poletto, *Biodesign in the Age of Artificial Intelligence: Deep Green*, Routledge, 2023.
7 Jan Boelen from Atelier Luma discusses this with the Lebanese architect taler Hashim Sarkis in this catalogue, pp. 70-75.
8 See also *Atelier LUMA, Bioregional Design Practices*, Luma Arles, 2023.
9 See the exhibition catalogue *Cecil Balmond: Frontiers of Architecture,* Louisiana Museum of Modern Art, 2007.
10 See pp. 130-137 of this catalogue. For more on 'Understanding the Rules of Life' see the US National Science Foundation at new.nsf.gov.

MARIO CARPO
For a start let's briefly introduce your background, your ambitions, your ideas. You are educators and academics. We've met many times, in various schools of architecture around the world: first I think, at Cornell University, some 15 years ago, then at the Architectural Association (AA) in London. Then we both came to teach at the Bartlett, University College London, where we are meeting today, and where we both teach. You are also tenured professors at the School of Architecture of the University of Innsbruck. So, we are colleagues in the sense that we are both academics and educators. But in addition, you are what I am not: professionals. You have an office, a practice where you design buildings, but you also design objects, and you design exhibitions and installations, including the installation which will support this exhibition. When did the practice ecoLogicStudio begin?

CLAUDIA PASQUERO
In July 2005.

MARCO POLETTO
We were in London, at the AA School of Architecture. We were doing different things: teaching, advising, working, all the kind of stuff you do.

MC
Because your first training was at the Polytechnic University of Turin, right?

MP
In Turin, yes, in 1998.

CP
We met waiting for an exam.

MP
Because she was PA, Pasquero, and I was PO, Poletto.

MP
We came to London in September 2001 with a mission to study architecture at a place like the AA, which we knew as being experimental, but I don't think we knew exactly what that meant. And the first few months were quite a shock because the education or pedagogical model was so radically different from the Polytechnic.

CP
But there were a few connections with our previous academic training. One was related to coding, which at the time was central to the research and teaching there. Additionally, some of the courses at the AA were related to this philosopher from Turin, Gianni Vattimo, who had embarked, when we were studying there, on a series of courses on the relationship between technology and philosophy. And connections were being made at Turin between technology, philosophy and aesthetics. Vattimo was interested in fostering a relationship with the Faculty of Engineering, although I remember the course was very small, basically just Marco and I.

MC
This is a good point because you studied at a polytechnical university and the tradition of polytechnic training in architecture connects to engineering, which studies inorganic materials.
Likewise, architects deal with bricks and stones. When we deal with timber, we deal with timber as a dead material. The timber we design and build with is not an organic material. It can still burn but it doesn't grow anymore. It's dead and gone.
And then we deal with artificial materials: steel and glass and iron, which we invented in the 19th century because

we needed them. All this falls into the realm of the inorganic, of minerals.

Whereas, in your practice, you deal with organic material, with biology and life, with plants and animals, which is rather unique in the domain of architectural experimentation. So, the question arises, how did you gather the technical background to deal with biology, which is a discipline we do not study in schools of engineering?

MP

The first approach did not directly involve living organisms. We went through a series of steps that involved computation.

That's where we started to engage with the matter of architecture as something that can possess a form of intelligence, if you will, or life or, in any case, it is not something to be shaped, a passive substance to be moulded but something that can have generative possibilities and potentials.

And this was very much the kind of agenda that we found at the AA. In the first ten years of the millennium, digital computation was really entering architecture. But at the same time, the AA had such a tradition of making models, of working with your hands as a craftsman.

So, as you can imagine, there were a whole bunch of new, experimental models where the model was no longer a macuette, a representational tool of something, again, shaped by our imagination but the model itself would be behavioural, alive in some sort of way, even without being biological.

CP

When I approached engineering, I loved mathematics and imagined I could apply it to a different kind of architecture.

And because of our interest in ecology, we started to work with plants that would develop ecological systems and there we realized there was a discrepancy between the mathematics, which can be very beautiful, and the brutality of the architecture to which it was applied and how the two came together.

And we said, okay, that's not possible and that's how we started to look for other paradigms that would allow us to better integrate the systems.

MC

This is illuminating. I've never thought of it in these terms, but for many in your generation, the transition from the inorganic to the organic didn't arise from philosophy or ecology or the environment, rather it came from computation.

Though computation is an inorganic tool, it brought you to deal with aspects of emergence and self-organisation which we typically attribute to organic life.

CP

This became critical for us when we were looking at projects from, for example Zaha Hadid. You could see that the project and the simulation was fluid.

I remember a presentation of the Hotel Puerta América, where Zaha presented the project, and it was deeply interesting how it was simulated and related to space. But at some point, the manufacturer came in and started to discuss how he very proudly moulded the Corian into a position it didn't want to hold. He was applying the latest engineering tools, and it was a beautiful project but, in our eyes, there was a discrepancy between how the project was simulated and how it was realised to millimetric precision, where the millimetric precision was probably not the central concept. So, we started to wonder whether there were processes, material processes, both synthetic and biological, that could allow a different transition from digital computation and simulation to the material world.

MC

And that was when complexity theory and various related theories of emergence and self-organization started to merge with computer science and with architectural theory, creating a conceptual framework that was – and still is – hugely relevant and inspirational for computational designers and designers at large. At the AA, the legacy of John Frazer – who has pioneered ideas of self-organization and cybernetic interactivity since the 1970s, when he collaborated with Cedric Price – created a fertile background for the rise of the Emergence and Design Group, founded in 2001 by Michael Weinstock, Michael Hensel and Achim Menges. The group authored several issues of *Architectural Digest (AD)*, of which the first, "Emergence: Morphogenetic Design Strategies", published in 2004, created a sensation at the time and is reportedly the best-selling issue in the history of *AD*.

CP

But it was not only emergent technologies. I was also in landscape urbanism, with Ciro Najle.

MP

The emergent technologies team probably pushed the connection with engineering the most. For example, Frei Otto became a popular figure because at the Stuttgart School, the institute of lightweight structures, he pioneered the idea of material computation as a way of simulating the behaviour of structural systems, rather than simply calculating their resistance. So, this suggested that form or morphology could emerge from a process of morphogenesis, and, in a sense, this introduced a generative perspective into design engineering.

MC

And at that point the connection with biology, the science of life, becomes inevitable.

MP

Yes, exactly. There is the so-called 'biomimetic' approach, which was a branch of engineering that used biological models to inform human artifacts. That's another way biology enters architectural design, let's say, from the engineering side.

MC

Biomimetics is old hat. It's a 19th century way of imitating nature.

MP

At the AA there were surely different sensibilities, for instance, some were more immersed in the discourse around landscape urbanism and in the living world of the gardener/landscaper rather than in the more abstract morphogenesis of engineering.

MC

So, that was the death knell of the old polytechnic view of the world whereby we design with inorganic materials, without knowing where they come from or caring about where they end up. We just design a chunk isolated from its source and destination.

This view of design and technology is not sustainable anymore, it's not a matter of philosophy and sensibility. It just does not work anymore. We cannot afford to do things that way because we will run out of energy, materials, etc. This mode of design has simply run into a wall. Now we know that the design of even the most specific and banal technical object must take into account the origin of the materials and where they will end up when the building is disassembled or the object is not used anymore.

We must take a holistic, comprehensive view, which some call circular, of the entire lifespan of the materials and the energy embedded in them. What 20 years ago was a philosophical view of the world is now a sociotechnical inevitability.

You intuited this and now we have to do what you started doing 20 years ago because that's the only way to conceive of design.

MP

Yes and no, I would say. I think the problem is that we still haven't gotten rid of the reductionist apparatus that controls most of the design disciplines.

What you're saying is true, but I don't think the way it is being done right now can be necessarily called holistic. We are doing the lifecycle assessment, we are doing the carbon neutrality assessment, we are doing all the certifications but this is all still done by chopping things into essentially tractable blocks, where the actual life in the cycle is completely absent and no one understands how that life may flourish or not in these new circular processes. It may be circular but still it is voided of life most of the time.

MC

It is still managed by engineers trained the traditional way.

MP

Yes. So, I think the battle is still hot and I think there is still a long way to go. And, funny enough, I would add that one of the main dissatisfactions that motivated us to work with new biological or living materials was the reductionist stance of environmental design itself.

On the one hand, we were deeply engaged in emerging design theories and so we were joining this explosion of morphogenetic processes and the complexity of forms and materialities. We felt these would lead us to a more profound paradigm of sustainable architecture.

But in the meantime, environmental design, which was growing considerably in scope, still applied the reductionist method of technical physics, the engineering of thermodynamic systems in the most basic form. For example in the idea of the zero-energy buildings.

MC

Because that's the mindset of the modern engineer. They can only quantify the inorganic and so they cannot deal with organic matter because that's how they were trained. This is the legacy of 25 centuries of architectural technology or of architecture as a technology.

Architecture has always been technologising nature. We build a house because we cannot sleep in the wilderness. So, we need technology as an alternative to nature.

MP

So, for us, introducing algae as a design material was a convenient way to subvert this approach. We did it with the intention of disruption, by using algae as a living material.

MC

Weeds.

CP

Microorganisms.

MP

Cyanobacteria. They were cool because on the one hand they were alive, so they disrupted the paradigm of environmental design related to ecology in a dead body, where materials had to perform in a certain way, which you could enter into a spreadsheet and then calculate the exact outcome and nothing would ever change.

At the same time, they were microscopic, so you couldn't treat them like little plants and flowers in the picturesque tradition of landscape architecture and that kind of garden composition.

MC

Exactly. That would be gardening.

MP

Exactly. So, they were essentially living pixels, converting solar radiation into a generative fabric of living architectures, from bit to pixel to cell. I remember talking to Brett Steele, who was director of the AA at the time. We showed him the first installation we did with algae. We had basically just collected algae from the canals of London, bottled them and created a wall of bottled algae. And he looked at the photo and he said, oh, that looks like pixelated nature. This sentence stuck with me because I thought, yes, exactly.

So, let's make a wall of pixelated nature where every pixel of the wall is alive, constantly changing. The density, transparency, translucency, transmission of heat and sun changes all the time and it indexes the variables of sun, of light, of people blowing into it, of change. So, all of a sudden, it becomes a living cyber-organic model where specific material properties and architectural design considerations influence this cycle of life.

CP

Integration is also an important issue. While many projects aim to be ecological, only a few truly integrate ecological processes into the design development. Instead, ecology often becomes a checklist rather than a core element of the design.

This approach to ecology is too abstract to meaningfully impact the day-to-day life of the contemporary urban dweller. For example, the process of carbon offsetting, despite its admirable goals, is mostly implemented in a disconnected manner, and the final impact is materially removed from the individual or institution that has initiated it.

MC

Yes. The idea of offset is you can take a plane if you also buy a tree.

MP

Yes.

CP

The system is so mechanical and disaggregated. It's not an ecological body.

MC

This is the legacy of the modernist polytechnical mentality. This is how we traditionally tackled the technological problem of architecture, by technologising nature. So, we cannot deal with timber as it is. In the polytechnic tradition we have transformed timber into something calculable. We cannot even deal with stones anymore, which is what artisanal, traditional culture always did because at the time there was no alternative.

CP

But the problem is not the stone, it's the artisanal culture, because architecture in these types of calculations needs to be standardised, repeatable, cannot be bespoke because bespoke is a luxury our society and culture can't afford. But, on the other hand, ecology cannot function in the standardised mechanical manner.

MC

We can only deal with an artificial stone, which we have designed for that purpose and we call it "concrete". Long ago we took boulders from nature and put them into a wall, but we cannot do that anymore because engineers cannot calculate it. Today you take the stone, bring it to a mill, bake it, cook it, smash it and convert it into concrete. Concrete has a huge carbon footprint.

This is the modern mechanical way of dealing with architecture as a technical tool. We technologise nature because that's the only way to notate it and to calculate it, and to fabricate things.

But we can do the opposite. Today, technology can, finally, try to naturalise architecture, which means dealing with a tree as it is, not with timber; dealing with a stone as you find it, not with concrete, etc.

MP

That's what we did, for example, in Tree One. We tried to make a provocation. The idea is that rather than engineering timber, let's reinvent the tree.

MC

Exactly.

MP

This piece is a tree that is robotically reprinted with biopolymer made of algae biomass that grows within the 3D printed structure. So, in a sense you have a new kind of tree made of cyanobacteria and robotic processes.

MC

You deal with trees. But you're not gardeners.

MP

No. We're architects, so we are naturalising architecture.

MC

You're naturalising and here we should mention Frédéric Migayrou of the Centre Pompidou in Paris, who came up with this expression and organized a memorable exhibition with that title. This was at the 9th ArchiLab exhibition at the FRAC in Orléans, which Migayrou co-curated with Marie-Ange Brayer in 2013.

MP

Of course. But it is also significant to us because we were part of that exhibition, which was very important to our trajectory.

MC

It was a turning point.

MP

It was a turning point. It was a significant moment for us.

MC

So you're not gardeners. You're not farmers either. You are architects. This brings me to what one of the most fascinating aspects of your recent work: the digital manipulation of photosynthesis.

In the exhibition we see some of your photosynthesis in vitro, photosynthesis recalculated, manipulated and artificially recreated. How does it work?

MP

Well, it works by designing new photobioreactor systems, essentially designing artificial habitats for microalgae organisms to grow within the fabric of architecture.

When that happens, photosynthesis and the apparatus

that sustains it become an architectural system. And so, you establish a symbiotic relationship between whoever inhabits the space and the space itself and the elements that fill it, such as light and air.

By controlling the flow of CO_2 and pollutants that are part of the urban atmosphere, and which we all breathe, and feeding that to the living cultures of cyanobacteria you can influence their growth. And when you influence their growth, this also influences yourself because they're growing next to you. And it influences the transparency, the colour of the space and also the possibility for you to grow biomass, biomaterial and nutrients to feed on.

MC

Nutrients because it is carbohydrates. We eat them.

MP

Exactly. We can eat them.

In the end, this idea of circularity is embedded. It's embedded in a spatial and architectural matrix and therefore it's never-ending. It's a cybernetic process that continues to evolve.

MC

You can control photosynthesis with an app.

MP

Exactly. You can interact with it.

CP

It's a different paradigm of control.

MP

We call it cyber-gardening because it's a form of gardening mediated by biodigital technologies, if you will.

CP

It aims to be a conversation rather than a means of control. It defines architecture slightly differently in its re-

lationship to the biosphere and the urbansphere or the wilderness and the human.

Nowadays the urbansphere is wilder than the biosphere. And maybe that's our hypothesis: we don't need an architecture to protect us from the biosphere. Rather, we need architecture that is softer, wetter, temporal, an ephemeral interface that enables us, through different tools, to converse with the urbansphere and the biosphere. It's a more dynamic form of control.

In that sense, computation, whether analogue or digital, becomes a means to interpret ecological processes. This enables us to develop architecture as a form of communication, supported by material and virtual pattern languages.

MC

You could say that whereas historically, technology has been applied to create an alternative to nature, today it is rather part of nature.

CP

Yes. It was a sort of barrier. It was sheltering.

MC

But at the same time you don't put flowers on the balconies, which is what many of our architect friends do, vertical walls, etc.

Flowers on the balcony encourages photosynthesis but this is not how you do it. You create a machine which is computationally controllable, which creates an artificial photosynthesis, which has an architectural shape, which is not organic but mechanic.

CP

We are not against flowers. We are currently distributing some medicinal flowers in Geneva. Computationally distributed. But we work with integrating microalgae because on a scientific level also we would like to start from the microbiome rather than from a large tree.

MP

Because the potential is much bigger.

CP

We are not looking at nature in an iconic manner, as a representation of lost beauty, but seek to establish a conversation. How do you speak with a flower? How do you speak with microalgae? To speak with a biological system or with planet Earth, we can make use of the support of computational systems or forms of artificial intelligence.

MP

One of the interesting things we are doing in Innsbruck at the Synthetic Landscape Lab, where our research is closer to landscape and therefore not just microorganisms but trees and plants and flowers and so on, is to push further the opportunities to draw nature digitally. This is because as a designer, as an architect, drawing is your tool to make sense of something that you want to bring into your design process. For example, initially with the algae it was possible to consider the alga as a pixel, a number and bring it into a certain type of computational process.

Now, we work with LiDAR scanning, with AI, these types of tools. It is possible, effectively, to begin to engage with macro and complex organisms like flowers and plants and, again, to go beyond the picturesque or symbolic idea of nature.

MC

Flowers and leaves.

MP

Yes, exactly. And to begin to work our way through essentially designing a new tree or synthesising a new tree from a more sophisticated application of design tools and digital tools to naturalising architecture, if you will. When it comes to flowers and trees, one of the workflows that we've developed starts from 3D scanning. In our research, we have developed a beautiful way to create a 3D scan of lichens, in extremely high resolution.

And then, from there, through AI, we are reconstructing almost as in a tomography, a kind of three-dimensional slicing which, again, it's not about recreating the complexity of the real thing because nature has already done this over millions of years of evolution. Rather it's about engineering a new relationship to the living.

MC

Exactly. Because some of your pieces, they're not trees, but a machine which does the same job but better.

MP

Yes. I think that calling it a machine is tricky though because for many people machines are mechanical things, and we are trying to reimagine a technological apparatus for architecture that does away with mechanical systems as much as possible. Of course, this is a gradual process. We cannot always jump three orders of magnitude and suddenly turn something that works at the scale of a pixel into a building.

MC

Perhaps we could call it soft machine, a design system.

MP

Yes. It's a design system that uses living organisms, 3D printed substrata capable of interacting with the living

organisms in more sophisticated ways through their formal articulation, through their material biochemical reaction and reactivity. We can build them at larger scale through robotic replication and other technologies.
And AI also creates the possibility to turn a simulation to a more speculative vision, so again the possibility to conceive of design itself as an evolutionary process. You don't aim at the final result. Rather you create a continuously renewing vision of what your project can become.

MC
If we look at the bigger picture, design is creating oxygen, eliminating carbon dioxide and producing food and carbohydrates.

MP
At a more basic level, this is an architectural carbon capturing and utilisation technology. Rather than building huge fans in the desert that suck up CO_2 and try to push it back underground, we build small biological devices that re-metabolise it into new architectures.

MC
This is what nature always did, but this designed piece is supposed to do it even better than nature.

MP
More efficiently and closer to where the most intense emissions are produced.

MC
Because we can microdesign it in a way that nature itself cannot do.

MP
Yes. In a sense, we are also dealing with the infrastructure of our cities and what we call the "urbansphere". The urbansphere is a human creation and so, when you try to embed a form of carbon capturing you have to work with its structures and systems.

MC
But you do not create a carbon sink. You use CO_2 to produce oxygen and carbohydrates.

MP
Exactly. It's a re-metabolisation process. You're adding a layer to the urbansphere that enables it to become more efficient in re-metabolising its own emissions.

MC
You don't do this by planting a tree at the corner of a street, but rather by designing a technical system.

MP
Yes. Even trees planted at the corner of a street could be part of a technical system if somebody actually designed it that way. In some of our urban design projects we have seen trees as an infrastructure. You can plant a thousand, or a million trees in a city as a new infrastructure, so that they are monitored, digitally controlled, have a specific distance, support networks of insects, birds, wildlife and proliferate.
In this sense, trees at a different scale, not an architectural scale but an urban scale, can be an infrastructure. At an architectural scale, trees are too big. Even when they are placed in these vast towers, they look picturesque and symbolic.
They have roots. They need lots of soil and you would need to have a million trees on a building with enough soil for their roots and the mycelium network to connect.

MC
The tree would have to be 100 times bigger than the building and at that point the building wouldn't function anymore.

MP

In my opinion, the buildings are currently too small for the trees to become a machine infrastructure and, on the other hand, for architecture, microalgae and microorganisms can efficiently re-metabolise it. That's why we're pushing for microorganisms in particular.

This is a question of resolution and scale, which comes from computational thinking and design. Normally, architects talk about scales of one to five, one to ten, one to one hundred. We talk about resolution because that's how you make sense, in cybernetic, computational terms, of the effects of an organism within a bigger infrastructural network or system.

MC

This technologises the micromanagement of photosynthesis, which is what you are unique in doing because other people would put a tree on the roof. Of course, you can put a tree on the roof. It just doesn't solve any problem. Whereas the micromanagement of a customisable photosynthesis is a technical system.

MP

The problem is that we ended up realizing this kind of idea would probably take three lifetimes to be developed. The reductionist approach, the engineering approach has such strong ties with the financial model that drives everything, which is essentially driven by simple numbers and basic equations. There is little space for the speculative engineering required to make this step.

CP

But the industry has started to take interest in ecology and circular systems, though still not in this symbiotic integration.

MP

Initially, I had this dream that photosynthesis could enter and transform the industry just as oil and other resources had, in an intense and powerful way that would automatically trigger the re-metabolisation of the building industry. We're certainly working on that every day so it's a reality for us.

CP

But it's a dilemma because even the introduction of AI and the way we deploy it more speculatively to connect data with the vision is quite divergent from how AI is implemented in everyday life.

MP

Well, because AI is implemented to make the cubic tomato, like precision agriculture, all these kinds of things that deploy AI, farming and so on.

MC

To optimise mass production.

MP

Yes. To push mechanical automation to the next level, turning the entire biosphere into a bigger assembly line of standardized, engineered components. That was the modernist project. It might have been a good idea a hundred years ago. It is certainly not a good idea now.

MC

Photosynthesis is the reversal of fire, it is fire in reverse. There is too much fire in the world, so to counteract fire we need more photosynthesis, and we need to design it, master it, to micromanage it, to customise it.

MP

Yes, because photosynthesis that exists naturally in the world is not enough.

Location
Humlebæk, Denmark

Year
2024

Deep.Forest celebrates the naturalisation of architecture and technology, a reversal of the modernist impulse to mechanise the natural world. Nature in all its cyber-organic variations can be discovered here in the networked paths of this exhibition.

Deep.Forest mirrors the natural variation in vegetation density surrounding the Louisiana, as captured by the machine eyes of the Copernicus and Sentinel 2 satellites. These observations are transformed into Digital Elevation Models and Normalised Difference Vegetation Index readings, creating a cyber-organic map of the local ecology that is brought to life in built form.

Deep.Forest gives architectural expression to the micromanagement of photosynthesis: 44 AIR.reactors host 500 litres of living algae cultures, capturing 600g of CO_2 per day from the atmosphere – the equivalent of a small, mature forest. The CO_2 is re-metabolised by the algae cells which produce 400g of biomass daily. The biomass is harvested, dried and converted into a biodegradable polymer for 3D printing. 20 3D printed biodegraders, scanned from 102 salvaged birch trunks, are covered in the algae-infused biopolymer. Their infill is made of 300kg of spent coffee grounds inhabited by colonies of living mycelium, which feed on the sugars in the coffee grounds until it fills all gaps, solidifying into a new, solid trunk. At the same time a carbon storage and a grown architectural component. There are five main paths in Deep.Forest, each exploring distinct research ecologies: GAN-Physarum, Habitat.ONE, Synthetic Landscape Lab, DeepGreen and H.O.R.T.U.S. Each pathway embodies a line of inquiry in ecoLogicStudio's bio-digital design practice.

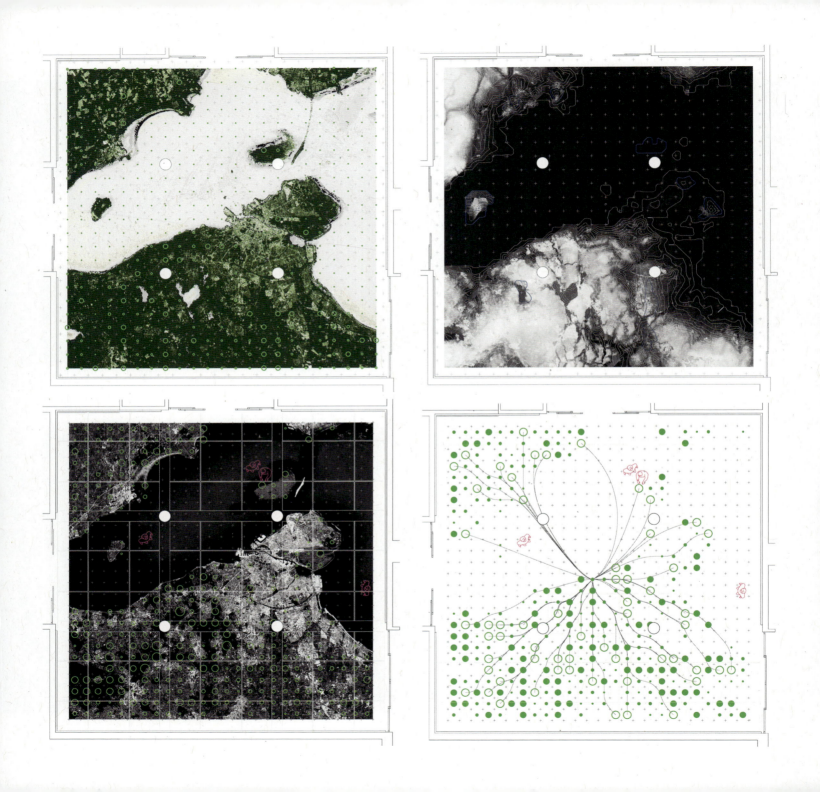

Deep Forest: cyper-organic map transposed to the exhibition gallery

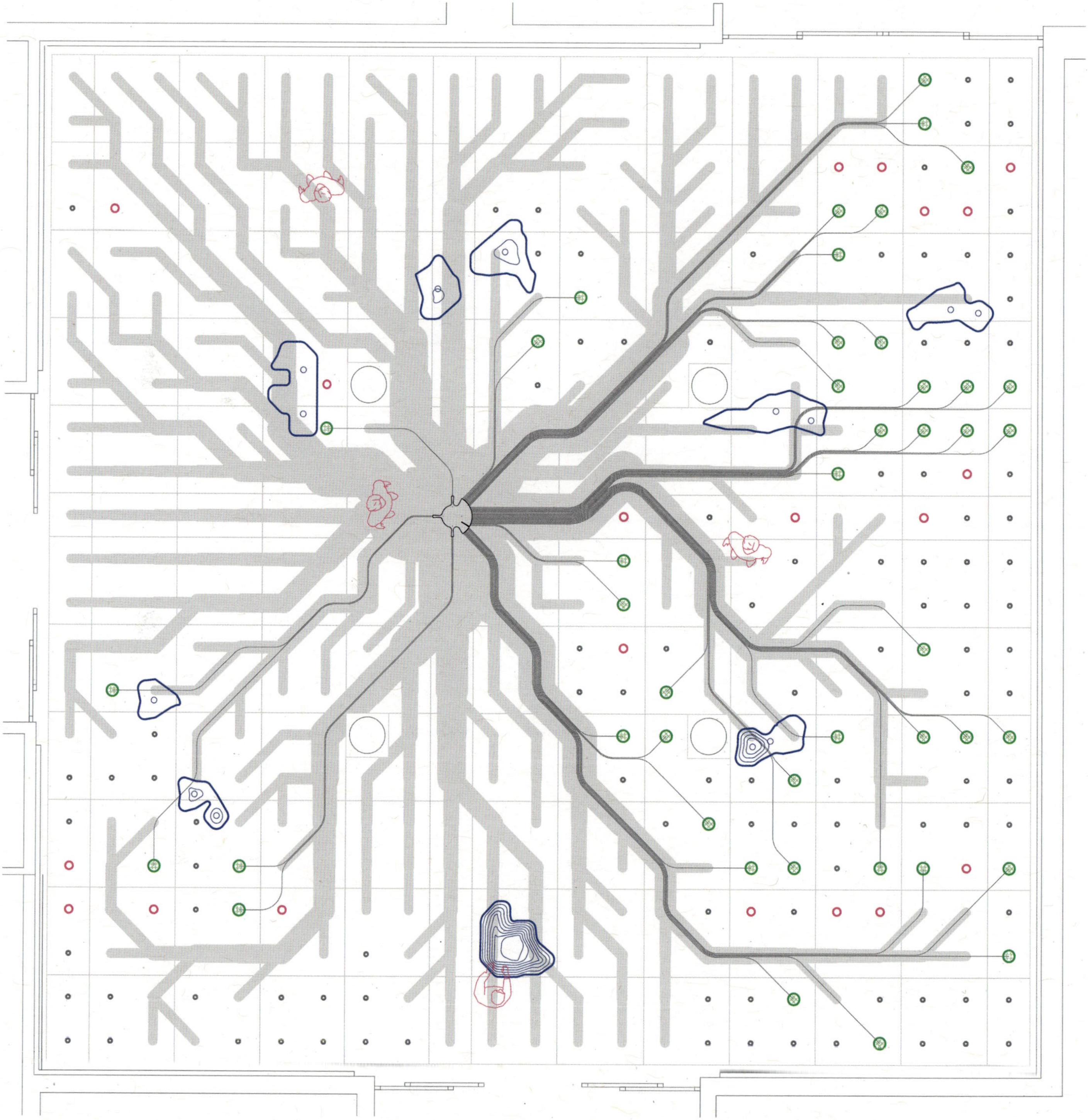

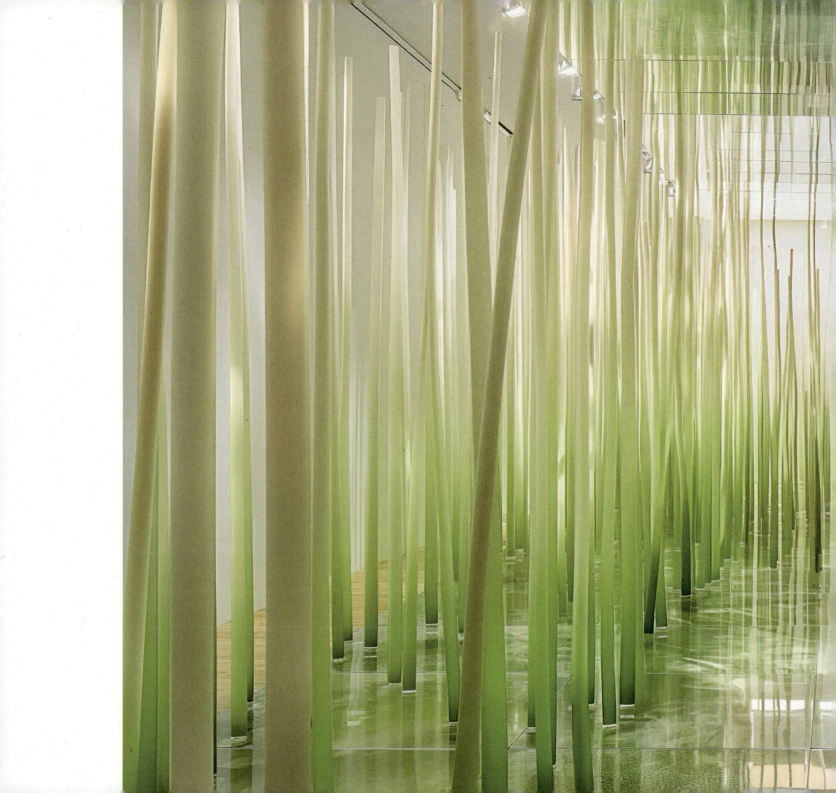

A GAN (generative adversarial network) is an algorithmic architecture that creates new generative models using deep learning methods. In this project a machine learning algorithm has been trained to 'behave' like a *Physarum polycephalum*, a single-celled slime mould, and asked to depict the future of a bio-digital autonomous Paris. The trained GAN-Physarum is sent on a computational dérive, an experimental drifting, on the streets of Paris. In an AI-generated video, it shows how to decode and reinterpret the patterns of contemporary Paris's urban fabric. We witness a transition from the original morphological order to an emergent distributed network of path systems: the blue-green, wet and living infrastructure of the city of the next millennium.

The video is accompanied by a corresponding bio-painting where a living *Physarum polycephalum* stretches its networked body to feed on a grid of nutrients, distributed on the canvas to accurately map the Parisian current biotic resources. The resulting traces are the embodiment of the slime mould's cognitive system and, perhaps, a non-human insight into Paris's very own evolving biotechnological brain.

A related project, DeepGreen: Urbansphere, explains in detail the workflow underpinning the GAN-Physarum algorithm and describes ecoLogicStudio's research into the application of artificial intelligence to develop new blue-green masterplans for contemporary cities. DeepGreen aims at designing systemic cities that use their size and collective energy to offer refuge for both humans and displaced wildlife that promote the emergence of positive microclimate, replenish depleted water sources and restore degraded terrains, pushing back on processes such as desertification, land erosion and contamination.

Location
Paris, France

Year
2021

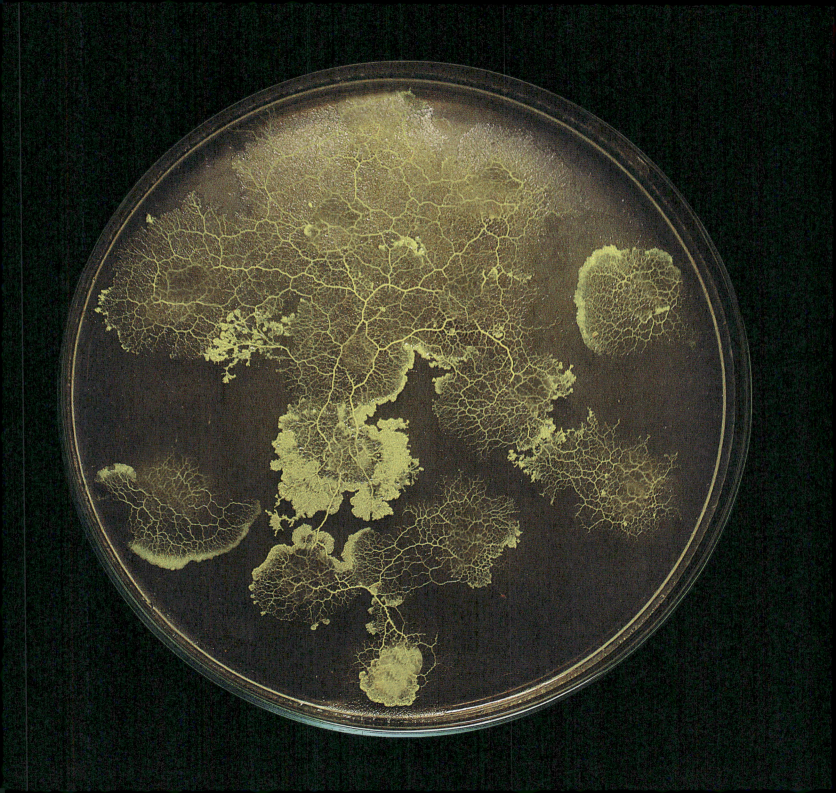

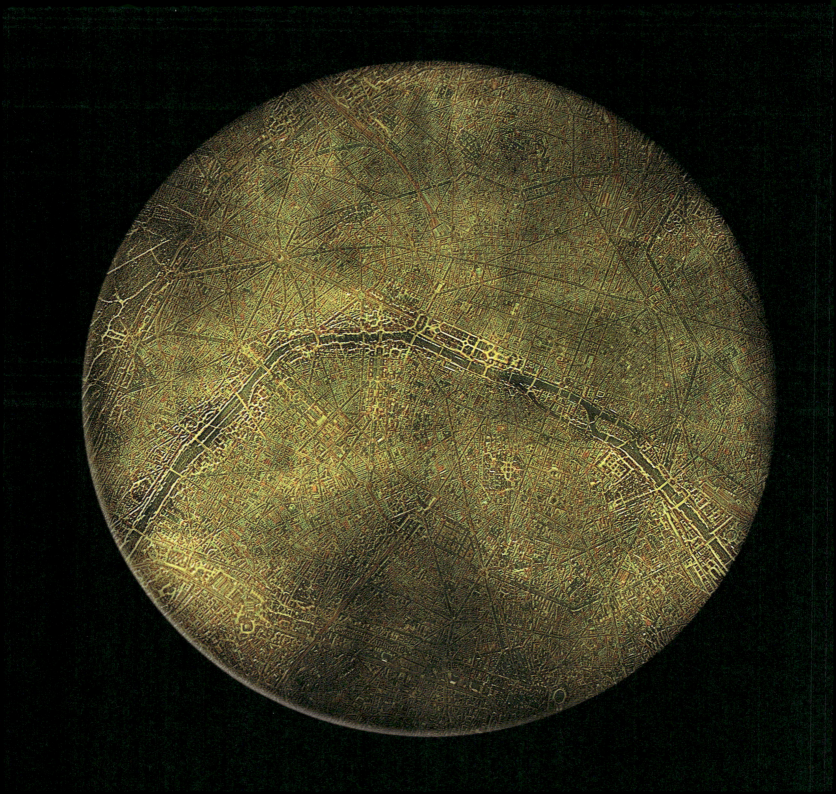

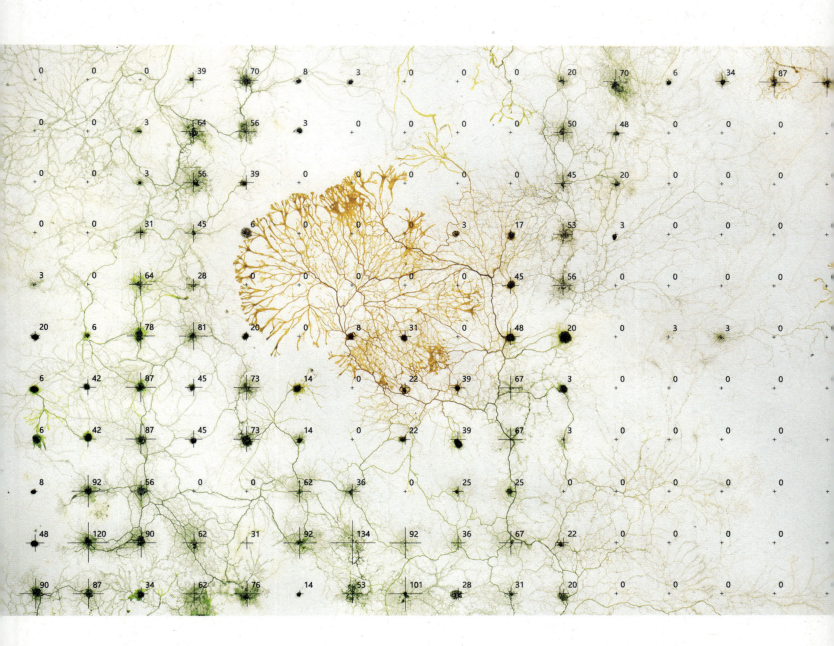

GAN-Physarium Paris
Growth: 20
Scale: 10 km
Building transformation: 15118

GAN-Physarium Paris
Growth: 70
Scale: 1 km
Building transformation: 55256

Tree One is a living carbon capturing sculpture designed by artificial intelligence and bio-digitally grown. Composed of three distinct components created through robotic printing – roots, trunk and canopy – the installation serves as a carbon capture mechanism by utilizing the cultivation of liquid microalgae within four intricately designed bioreactors. These bioreactors are seamlessly integrated into the intricate venous structure of the trunk component. The sculpture re-metabolises and stores the carbon molecules into its trunk and canopy while releasing oxygen in the atmosphere. The Tree One exhibited at the Hyundai Motorstudio Seoul integrates 40 glass photobioreactors hosting 500 liters of living cyanidium algae cultures. These can capture as much carbon dioxide as 12 large trees, the equivalent of a small urban forest. The main structure of Tree One is designed by algorithms whose recognition of arboreal systems negotiates the architectural logic of the column. The trunk is made entirely from algae-based biopolymers and its strength derives primarily from its unique pleated structure inspired by the fibrous trunk of real trees. Its construction was made possible by a pioneering robotic 3D printing process.

Bio Lab showcased the process of bio-digital synthesis of Tree One and of the carbon neutral city. Designed as an open laboratory, the Bio Lab presents the proprietary bio-design innovation that was developed to create Tree One.

Client
Hyundai Motor Company

Location
Seoul, Korea

Year
2023

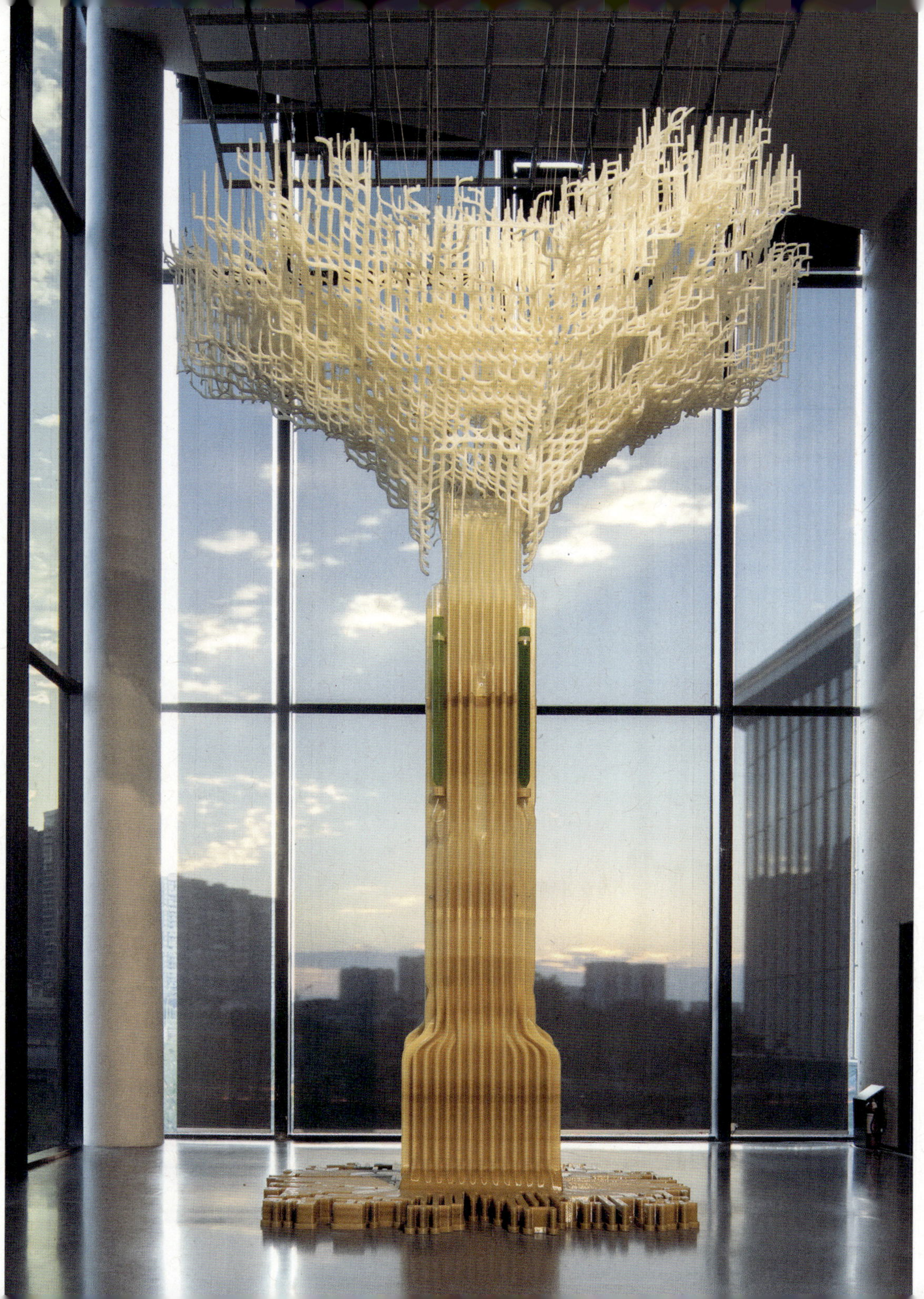

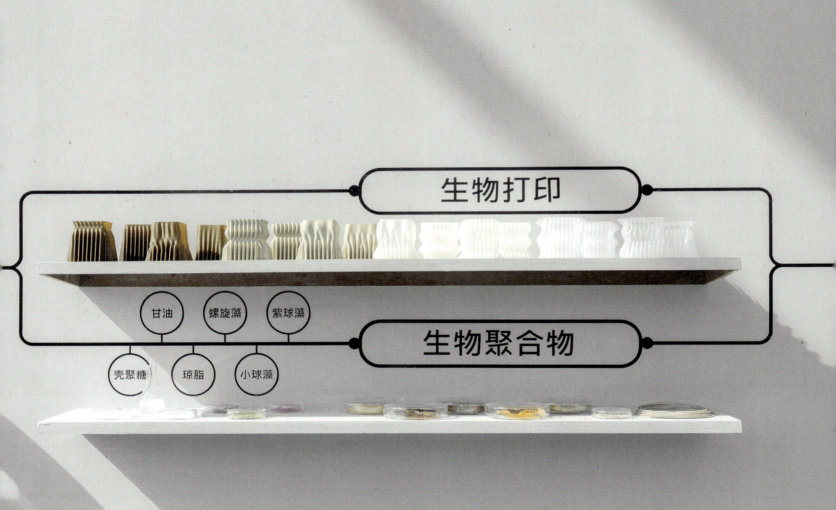

生物打印

生物聚合物

甘油　螺旋藻　紫球藻

壳聚糖　琼脂　小球藻

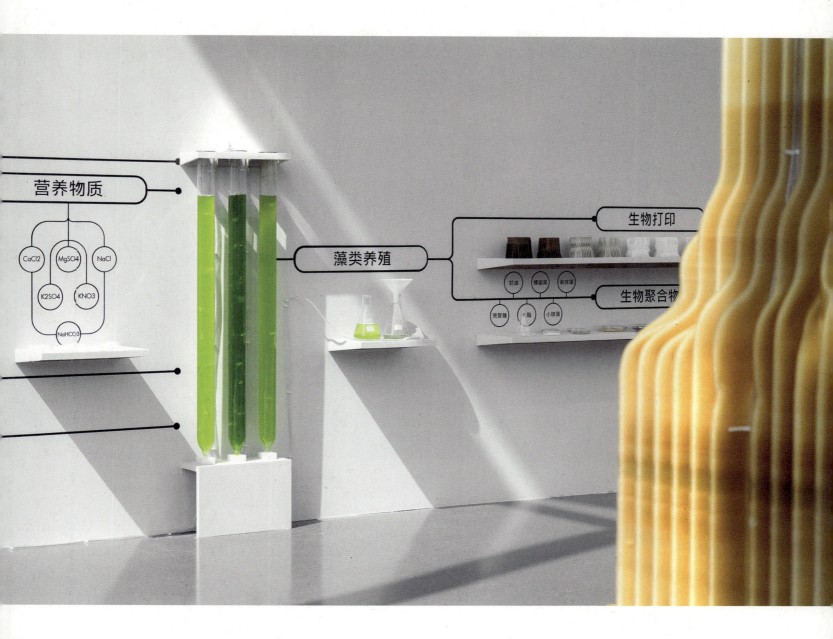

营养物质

CaCl2　MgSO4　NaCl

K2SO4　KNO3

NaHCO3

藻类养殖

生物打印

生物聚合物

甘油　螺旋藻　栅球藻

壳聚糖　脂　小球藻

AirBubble is a playground that integrates air-purifying micro-algae in the centre of Warsaw. The purifying process is powered by solar energy and children's playfulness. The playground integrates photosynthesis in the built environment through the Photo.Synth.Etica technology invented by ecoLogicStudio. AirBubble is an urban algae greenhouse built up by a cylindrical timber structure wrapped in an ETFE membrane that protects 52 glass algae reactors. The ETFE membrane controls the microclimate inside AirBubble, while the inverted conical roof enhances air recirculation and natural ventilation, helping to maintain a clean and healthy play area.

The AirBubble monitoring system integrates urban air pollution sensors and is connected to a data processing platform capable of comparing measurements in real time and of highlighting the Air Quality Index for six core pollutants: fine particulate PM2.5 and PM10, ground level ozone (O_3), nitrogen dioxide (NO_2), sulphur dioxide (SO_2) and carbon monoxide (CO). AirBubble is capable of absorbing 97% of the nitrogen and 75% of particulate matter from the air. Early data collected in May 2021 showed that PM2.5 concentrations within the playground have fallen well within the recommended WHO limits (green zone, AQI below 20). The peak reduction rate was 83%. This figure has been calculated by comparing readings from an external pollution sensor with real-time data feeds from a monitoring device inside AirBubble.

The AirBubble hosts 52 large bioreactors in borosilicate glass, each containing 520 litres of living green *Chlorella sp.* algae cultures that can filter a flow of polluted air of 200 litres per minute. While the liquid medium flushes away particles, the algae actively eat polluting molecules and carbon dioxide, releasing fresh clean oxygen in return.

Client
Otrivin Breathe Clean

Location
Warsaw, Poland

Year
2021

BioBombola is a pioneering project that invites individuals, families and communities to cultivate a domestic algae garden as a sustainable source of vegetable protein. BioBombola absorbs carbon dioxide and oxygenates homes more effectively than typical houseplants while fostering a fulfilling daily interaction with nature. During the Covid lockdown, ecoLogicStudio cycled everyday with their two children between their home and their bio-lab in London's East End. Spontaneously, they involved the whole family in algae cultivation and in air pollution data collection. Inspired by this experiment, ecoLogicStudio developed the BioBombola as a simple indoor cultivation kit. Each BioBombola kit includes a harvesting system for fresh spirulina, a nutrients bag and a starter batch of spirulina cells. It is composed of a single customized photobioreactor: one-metre tall glass container, filled with 15 litres of living photosynthetic spirulina strain and culture medium with nutrients. It also includes an air piping system and a small air-pump that constantly stirs the medium. The gentle bubbling keeps the algae afloat, aids oxygenation and produces a calming sound, releasing fresh oxygen into the surrounding environment.

The photobioreactor absorbs as much CO_2 as two young trees and produces the same amount of oxygen as seven indoor plants. Harvesting is simple and engaging, allowing up to one tablespoon of Spirulina per day, which is the daily recommended intake for a family of four.

The project explores a visual and tactile way to introduce high-tech cultivation into the urban context, encouraging hands-on interaction with nature in everyday life.

Location
London, England and Innsbruck, Austria

Year
2018-

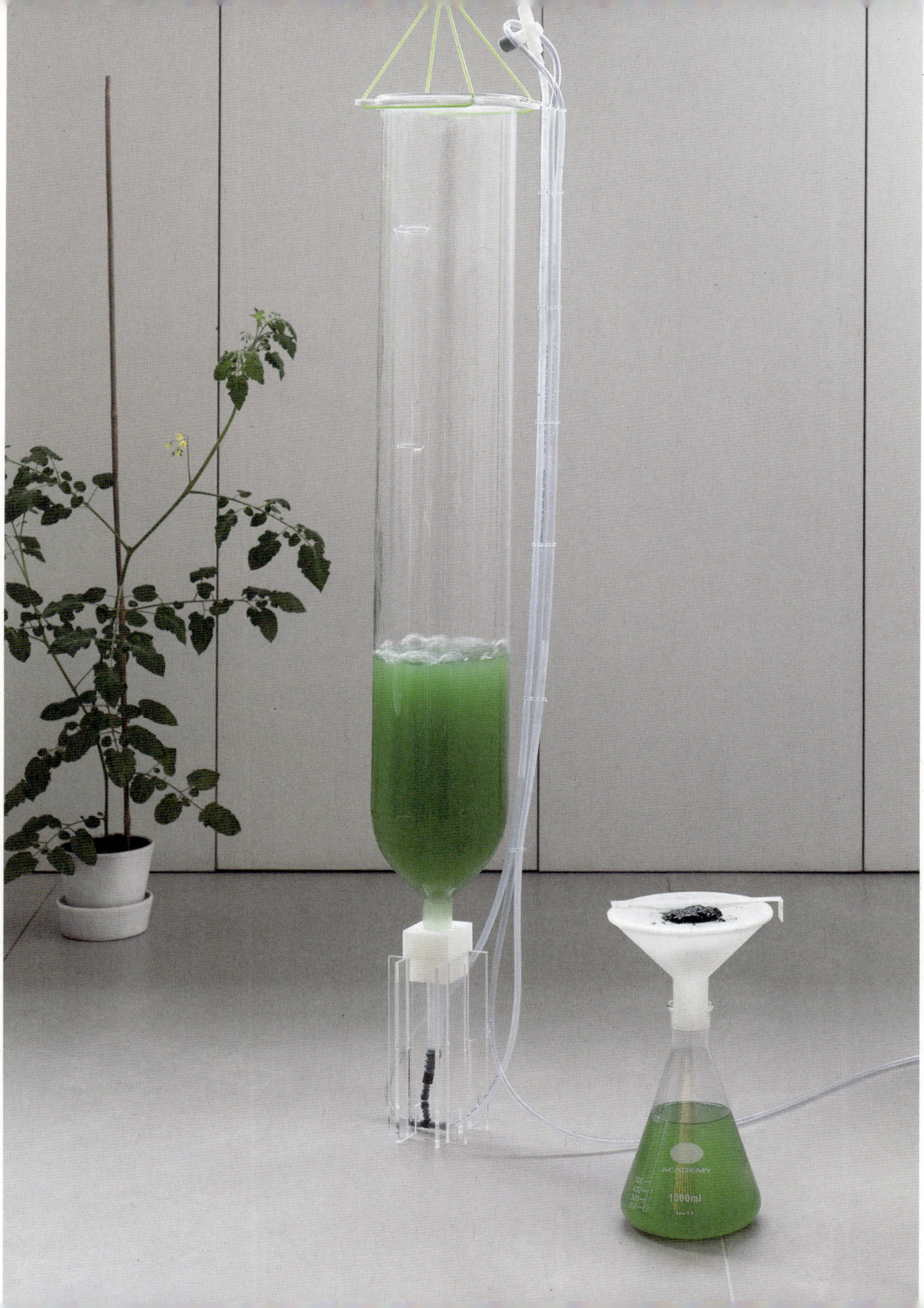
ACADEMY
1000ml

Client
Centre Pompidou, Paris, France

Location
Paris, France and Innsbruck, Austria

Year
2020

H.O.R.T.U.S. XL Astaxanthin.g is a large scale, high-resolution, 3D printed bio-sculpture receptive to both human and non-human life. In the digital era new interactions are emerging between creativity and the fields of life science, neuroscience and synthetic biology. The notion of 'living' takes on a new form of artificiality. This project challenges the dictates of human rationality by exploring the effects of proximity to bio-artificial intelligence. It is developed in 'collaboration' with living organisms, whose non-human agency is mediated by spatial structures inspired by biological models of endosymbiosis. A digital algorithm simulates the growth of a substratum inspired by collective coral morphogenesis. This is physically deposited by 3D printing machines in layers of 400 microns, supported by triangular cells of 46 mm and divided into hexagonal blocks of 18.5 cm. Photosynthetic cyanobacteria are inoculated on a biogel medium into the triangular cells, or bio-pixels, serving as the system's units of biological intelligence. Their metabolisms, powered by photosynthesis, convert radiation into oxygen and biomass. The density of each bio-pixel is digitally computed in order to optimally arrange the photosynthetic organisms along iso-surfaces that receive increased incoming radiation. Among the oldest organisms on Earth, cyanobacteria's unique biological intelligence is gathered to form a new kind of bio-digital architecture.

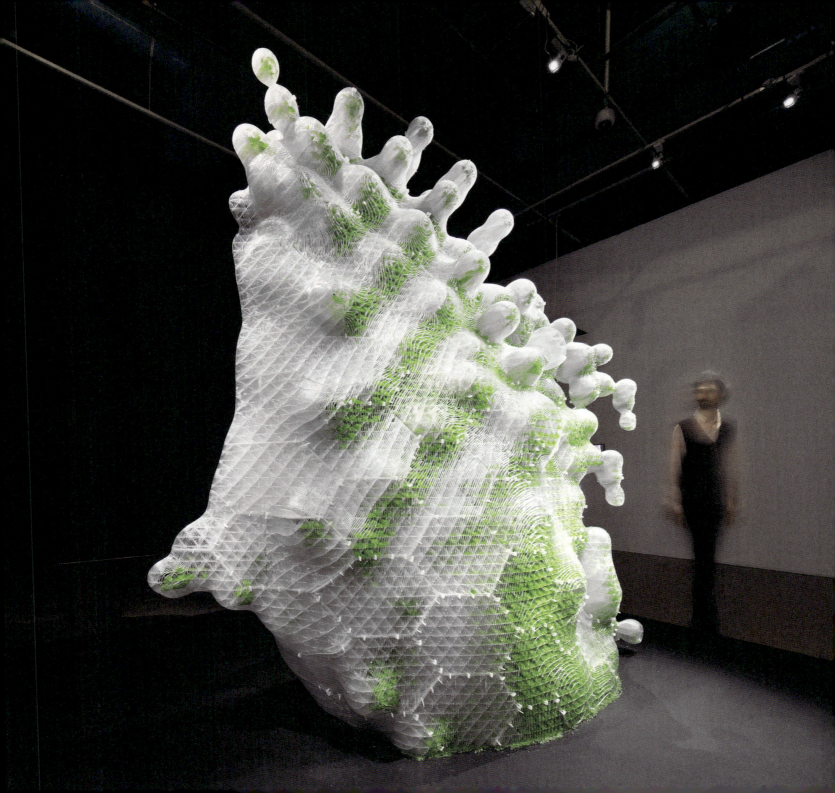

Location
Dublin, Ireland

Year
2018

Conceived as an 'urban curtain', Photo.Synth.Etica, captures CO_2 from the atmosphere in real-time, about one kilo of CO_2 per day, equivalent to that of 20 large trees. Composed of 16.2 × 7 metre modules, the curtain prototype envelopes the first and second floors of the Printworks building facade at Dublin Castle. Each module functions as a photobioreactor: a digitally designed, custom-made bioplastic container that utilizes daylight to feed the living micro-algal cultures and emits a luminescent glow at night.

Unfiltered urban air enters at the bottom of the Photo.Synth.Etica facade. As air bubbles naturally rise through the bioplastic photobioreactors, they come into contact with voracious microbes. CO_2 molecules and air pollutants are captured and stored by the algae, and grow into biomass. This can be harvested and used to produce bioplast, the primary material for the photobioreactors. Freshly photosynthesized oxygen is released at the top of each unit of Photo.-Synth.Etica, and improving the urban microclimate.

Thanks to their serpentine design, the modules optimise the carbon sequestration processs, while the curtain pattern evokes a large trading data chart that embodies Climate-KIC's commitment to innovative climate solutions. The system could be integrated into both existing and newly designed buildings. Smart cities, smart homes, autonomous vehicles, robotic factories, dominate the current panorama of popular futuristic scenarios, but they all need spatial and architectural re-framing to engender beneficial societal transitions.

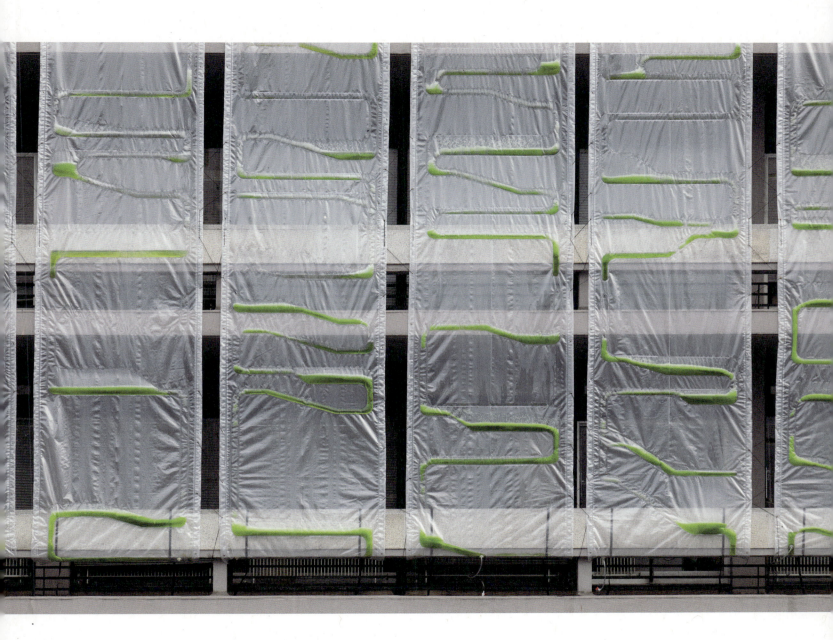

This project explores the intersection of land art, environmental science and territorial sustainability, focussing on the Alpine region. The primary goal is to understand the effects of climate change and human activities on the landscape while promoting the development of biodegradable materials that support landscape restoration and biodiversity.

Researchers are utilizing advanced mapping technologies and satellite monitoring to analyze human-induced transformations in the Alpine region, giving particular attention to soil humidity and water flow patterns and the growth of microalgal colonies, which serve as indicators of ecological change. This data helps in understanding the current state of the landscape, especially concerning melting glaciers. Inspired by the unique qualities of the Alpine microbiome, the project employs 3D-printing technologies to create sculptural pieces made from biodegradable polymers derived from the landscape itself, as substitutes for conventional plastics. These designs are intented to biodegrade back into the environment, transforming waste into nutrients for the landscape.

In the Anthropocene era, it is crucial to seek a non-anthropocentric mode of reasoning and designing. At the Synthetic Landscape Lab, this involves probing into the flow of energy, matter and information between the biosphere and the urbansphere, and exploring the interdependence of digital and biological intelligence in design by working directly with non-human agents such as AI and living organisms. The research examines the diagrammatic capacity of living organisms, coupled with machine intelligence, to contribute to the development of complex bio-digital architectures. This shift from linear to circular design, and from a human-oriented environment to a co-evolutionary symbiotic system, is key. Training designers to recognize patterns of reasoning across disciplines, materiality and technological regimes expands the aesthetic possibilites of design practice.

Location
Innsbruck and Obergurgl, Austria

Year
2017

Location
Centre Pompidou, Paris, France

Year
2018

In XenoDerma, spider web morphogenesis is intercepted with a man-made spatial scaffolding, algorithmically designed and 3D printed. Spiders' minds, in this case Asian fawn tarantulas, do not entirely reside in their bodies, as their webs constitute a form of spatial thinking. Information from their webs become an integral part of their cognitive systems. The behaviour of the spiders and the production of silk is re-programmed in XenoDerma through the design of the 3D printed substructure and of its geometrical features. The result intentionally embraces ambiguity, revealing, in the alien beauty of its silky morphologies, an intelligence that resides somewhere at the intersection of the biological, technological and digital realms.

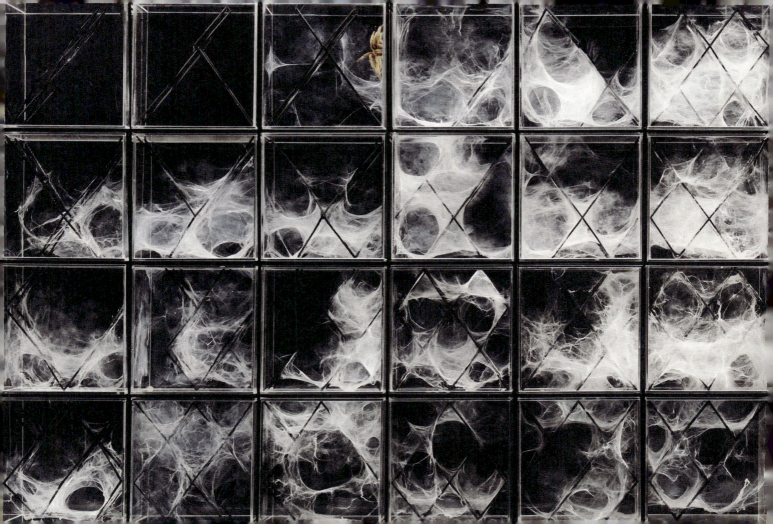

HASHIM SARKIS
Can you tell us about the exhibition at Louisiana Museum of Modern Art and your work at Atelier LUMA?

JAN BOELEN
At Atelier LUMA, we practice bioregional architecture. Rather than focussing on a single project, this exhibition presents a methodology. We explore what we currently define as "bioregioning" – how do you observe a region, identify its resources and connect them through design? How can these resources be implemented effectively, and how can the knowledge gained be shared with others?

Each chapter of the exhibition is illustrated with small case studies from Arles. For Humlebæk, which is where the museum is located, we present projects using local materials from the region. For instance, we make light switches from local industrial leftovers and produce an Arne Jacobsen chair from the veneer of an unwanted invasive tree that grows nearby.

Additionally, we repurpose museum paper, mixing it with materials such as algae sourced from the nearby sea, to create a pulp. From this, we 3D print bricks, demonstrating a unique blend of materials. These examples highlight what we've achieved in Arles and how we can continue to apply these principles.

HS
Let's start with the definition of "bioregional". Your work builds on a long legacy of thinking about bioregionality and biodiversity in the Camargue in the Southern France. How does your approach relate to the preservation efforts in this region, and how do you move from understanding the bioregion as a physical space to using it as a design strategy?

JB
In 2016, concepts like "footprint" and "circular thinking" weren't at the forefront. We began within the context of the LUMA cultural institute, which has roots in the Camargue's Tour du Valat, initiated by the Hoffman family, a research centre focussed on conserving Mediterranean wetlands. Initially, our approach was simple – bringing students to collect local materials and explore the ecosystem. Over time, we realized that these materials had deeper ecological roles. Fast-growing reed needed to be harvested at precise times to support local bird populations and capture carbon. Salt, which made the soil salty, also nurtured unique species, including algae with specific qualities. This led us to explore new materials and potential applications from the local landscape.

HS
How did this exploration of local ecosystems shape your understanding of design's role within a bioregional approach?

JB
Through working with many of these resources, we came to see that this wetland – an ecotone between sea and land – has a unique combination of biodiversity and climatological conditions. Design plays a key role in enhancing this. We can blend traditional skills with modern

science and technology, not to exploit the resources but to improve and sustain them. Eventually, I realized we weren't just a material lab; we were a bioregional design lab. The goal became creating local solutions with global applications by combining human and natural resources in thoughtful, sustainable ways.

Just as science offers a universal approach, we often see results in isolated laboratory conditions. But once you apply them in the real world, within a specific bioregional context, they must be adapted to fit that environment.

HS

As you develop your lab's work, how do you navigate the tension between regional approaches and global, standardized solutions? Can you give an example of where this tension creates challenges?

JB

There is definitely a conflict between these approaches. The push for universal solutions, like 'one-size-fits-all,' often leads to monocultural environments – whether it's the same crops, air conditioning or lighting standards everywhere. This standardization can block innovation and diminish biodiversity. While industrialization has brought global materials like concrete and steel, I don't oppose these materials. Instead, I believe we should combine them with local resources and rethink how we use what's available today. Fully rejecting modern materials would be nostalgic and unproductive; it's about integrating them meaningfully with local contexts.

HS

I've noticed that bioregionalism in your work focusses heavily on biodiversity, not cultural, geological or linguistic aspects of the region. How does this specific focus shape your approach?

JB

Our approach does start with biodiversity and culture because it forms the foundation of any bioregional strategy. We don't aim to essentialize the region but rather build from the biological realities present in the ecosystem. From there, we explore how these natural and cultural systems can influence design and materials, integrating technology and global solutions while respecting the region's unique ecological condition.

HS

I think much of this conversation is about the tensions between a regionalist approach and the universalist approach. Does this distinction also relate to the regional versus global approach?

JB

Yes, absolutely.

HS

Especially since you are directly working with design components that significantly contribute to global carbon emissions. For instance, we've discussed potential collaborations in areas like textiles and building materials, two industries that are major contributors to carbon emissions. By addressing these specific sectors, we are directly targeting carbon reduction. But there are many ways to do that. The biodiversity-driven, or bioregional approach is one. Let's talk a little bit about that. What are some other approaches, and why is the bioregional approach preferable?

JB

For example, if we consider the construction and textile

industries — two of the biggest contributors to carbon emissions — there's an enormous pollution footprint. You might think, "Let's solve everything with one solution." Suppose we started using algae tomorrow – for insulation material, for textiles and so on. Algae grows quickly, in as little as three weeks, and absorbs enormous amounts of carbon. Plus, it can help clean polluted waters.

It sounds like I've given you the perfect solution for our current problems. But if we commit fully to a single solution, that's the kind of mindset that has led us to the issues we're dealing with today. It's the same logic of monoculture – standardizing everything around one 'ideal' solution – that can cause new problems. If we mandated that everyone builds, produces and wears algae-based products tomorrow, we'd just create another monoculture, repeating the mistakes of the past.

That's why we need to consider the entire ecosystem and focus on biodiversity. There are many solutions available, and the key is to connect them with the right challenges, fostering diversity in our approach. If we scale these solutions to match specific bioregions – looking at local resources, population and environmental factors – we can address issues in a way that's tailored to each region. Although we're not fully there yet, using data to manage local resources and production could lead to a healthier, more sustainable world.

HS

You mentioned scaling up solutions, which leads me to my next question. How do we scale a solution to address climate issues without creating a new monoculture, which could end up harming the environment? We've talked about sunflower stems for sound panels as an example.

If you try to scale that up, there aren't enough sunflowers in the region, and growing more could create the same monocultural problem. So, how do you scale a solution like this to have a wider impact, without causing environmental harm, especially if global industries want to adopt it? Is that the right kind of scaling? In other words, how do we make sure that your innovative solutions, when expanded beyond their initial scope, continue to make the right impact?

JB

We can't have sunflowers everywhere, and even in a region like Arles you probably won't be able to produce enough acoustic panels from the sunflower. But, in fact, it's not just about the sunflower – it's about how you bring fibres together in a certain way. We've made acoustic panels from rice, thermal insulation from rice and sunflower acoustic panels.

Once you understand how acoustics work and the role fibres play, you work with what you have. Of course, the industry wants to scale up, but materials are heavy and should stay local, while people and ideas are light and should travel.

We sell our recipes to partners worldwide and help them adapt to their local situation. It's not a copy-paste method, it's a question of adaptation to the environment and to specific buildings and projects. When we partner with others, we set requirements for their local production and maintain an ongoing relationship to ensure these values are upheld.

HS
I think part of what you are doing with the Louisiana exhibition is showing how ideas can travel and be adapted to different materials and industrial contexts. In these early experiments that you're doing in Denmark, France and other places around the world, can you reflect on the challenges but also the promises of this translation process?

JB
The first challenge is convincing the commissioner. Once they see and feel the materials, they get very enthusiastic. It's revealing because when people visit Atelier LUMA, they're often convinced and want to do the same thing in their own context.

HS
But do they sometimes come back, and say, "We can't do that here"?

JB
Yes but actually we can. It's possible in most contexts.

HS
To dwell a bit longer on creating new materials from different regions' biodiversity, could you talk about what kind of infrastructure or regional mindset it takes, what are the motivations, production facilities and possible partners needed?

JB
We have also worked in the Middle East, in Sharjah, where we started from another point of view, from craft, but there's also a deep understanding of sustainability there. In the Middle East sustainability is not just a way of dealing with climate change; it's a matter of survival. It's driven by economic concerns, like preparing for a future without oil, and by the necessity of dealing with extreme heat. Sometimes, it starts small, with people who are curious, and then the right projects and energies come together. We see this happening in cultural projects, like in Korea, where we were invited to a biennial and got the chance to renovate a house, developing textiles, bricks and panels specifically for it.

There are also collaborations with industries tied to agriculture, like the wine industry in France. They understand that their current methods – how they harvest and produce wine – will be viable for the next 10, 20 or 30 years, so they're thinking long-term.

HS
How do you connect agriculture to both the food and building industries, and are there cases, where you move from working with the product itself to drawing inspiration from how products grow. Also, have you worked with animals at LUMA, or is it primary plants?

JB
Animals are a very important part of the story.

HS
There's a distinction between biological materials and biologically inspired ones. I feel that Atelier LUMA is more immersed in biology itself, whereas architecture often draws from biologically inspired ideas. Can you talk about the difference between those two approaches? Also, could you speak about the connection between plants and animals, since your work started with birds?

JB
We're not interested in mimicking nature's forms; our focus is on understanding biological processes and what

we can learn from them. It's not about imitating these processes but about starting with something like algae, which, for example, turns pink when stressed by salt. Plants and animals aren't really separate – they're interconnected. Take flamingos, for instance: they're pink because they eat pink algae, which thrive in salty environments. If the climate changes, flamingos won't stay pink. In a way, you can 'read' the weather by looking at a flamingo's colour. Everything is connected. Similarly, the sheep here – much like the goats in Lebanon – play a crucial role in maintaining the landscape by grazing on the grass and preventing wildfires from spreading. You can't separate plants from animals; they're all part of a larger, interconnected ecosystem.

HS

You mentioned sheep, which are central to your work in textiles and how you're trying to scale down in order to scale up, which I find to be a very beautiful solution. But birds, like flamingos, are transregional. How do birds, travelling across regions, influence your localized solutions? What do they carry with them that we can benefit from?

JB

A great example is Parc des Ateliers. It was almost a mineral desert until Bas Smets, the landscape architect, added a garden and a pond. He said, "Let's measure the success of my garden by the amount of birds that will be here." Now you see what the birds have brought: seeds, frogs and fish – creating their own environment. This interaction is crucial, and if we don't have these places, ecosystems will just disappear.

HS

So birds bring seeds from other bioregions, showing that a bioregion isn't a closed system?

JB

Exactly, it's an open system.

HS

This also challenges the notion of indigeneity in the bioregional approach. You talked about ideas travelling and people travelling, and so do birds and some species. While this can be a contentious issue for preservationists, do you see a future where bioregional thinking might include moving species, like growing more algae or sunflowers in Denmark to help solve some of the problems here.

In other words, can bioregional thinking involve carrying seeds from one place to another?

JB

Yes, I think so.

HS

Preservationists are very cautious about this.

JB

They are, and it is a concern. But with climate change, vegetation and plant species are already shifting.

HS

So, they are moving anyway.

JB

Exactly.

HS

One example might be the Shouf, the biosphere reserve in Lebanon, I am working on as an architect, where the tree line is rising. What are your thoughts on this?

JB

Yes, the tree line is moving upward, and wine production will shift to cooler areas. This is all happening, and while we can try to mitigate it, we can't be naive and ignore reality. We can't simply replant these trees lower and pretend nothing has changed. The bioregion is not like a fixed administrative border; it's a porous, dynamic zone that constantly evolves, much like culture itself. What seems stable is actually a flexible system that is continuously rebalancing itself. And I think that this dynamic nature is what makes it interesting and open to ongoing interaction.

HS

A very beautiful concept comes from early human geography, where one of the late 19th-century French geographers Paul Vidal de la Blache coined the term "possibilism". He argued that what a region gives us is possibilities, rather than dictating solutions, and it's up to us to make the choices. This interaction of possibilities and constraints fuels creative thinking in biodiversity approaches.

So, I want to ask about the connection between science and art in this context? Your work is making an impact through biennales, exhibitions and projects like the show at the Louisiana. Art plays a role in demonstrating, experiencing and translating these ideas. Can you elaborate on the current relationship between Atelier LUMA and the LUMA museum, and what you envision for the future?

JB

Atelier LUMA embodies the organic essence of the values and missions carried by LUMA Arles, which favour interdisciplinarity, research, creation and collaboration, while being deeply rooted in a specific area. I think art and other disciplines, like architecture and design, have the power to showcase alternatives in unique and varied ways. Cultural institutions can be a place to present and share these possibilities. I believe we're facing a crisis of imagination in society today. Beyond the political crises, wars and environmental challenges, what we need most is cultural change. We need to cultivate kindness – not just among ourselves, but towards everything around us. It may sound romantic, but I think we need this kindness in order to move forward. Cultural institutions, along with educational ones, play a crucial role in fostering this change. The ambition for our own building, Magasin Électrique, was to create a prototype that would enable the testing and application of this low-impact, locally-based bioregional approach at scale. The building needed to facilitate, encourage and expand on the ambitions of Atelier LUMA, presenting a new perspective on both design and materials, while promoting and highlighting innovation through bioregional design practices.

HS

Montaigne once wrote that of all the values in Aristotle's ideal city, friendship was the highest, even above justice. I'm happy that we're ending on the proposition that we return to that, emphasising the need to extend friendship to other beings on this planet. And I think in doing that, we're exercising our imagination at its most generous. My friend, thank you so much.

JB

Thank you.

In 2019, Atelier LUMA began collaborating with BC architects & studies and Assemble on the Lot 8 Project, a renovation of Le Magasin Électrique, which is located in the Parc des Ateliers. This building serves as a prototype for architecture that emphasises traditional know-how, collective on-site experiments and the development of materials rooted in the Arles bioregion. By spring 2023, Le Magasin Électrique had become the centre of Atelier LUMA's activities.

The ambition was to create a building that tests and scales a low-impact, bioregional approach. It aimed to support and expand Atelier LUMA's vision by offering new perspectives on both design and material use, while promoting innovation through bioregional practices. In alignment with Atelier LUMA's ongoing initiative "Building for Uncertainties", the concept of uncertainty became a key theme in the building's conception. Nearly 20 unique building applications were introduced in Le Magasin Électrique, including salt crystal door handles, structural rammed earth made from demolition waste and acoustic and hard paneling made from agricultural by-products.

A key element of this approach was the involvement of local actors engaged in various aspects of the project. Many of the materials used, from development to construction, were created in tandem with these local specialists. When certain expertise was unavailable locally, we worked to make partnerships between local and international teams to ensure knowledge transfer and collaboration.

Location
Parc des Ateliers, Arles, France

Year
2023

Interior

The interior plan is organized into three main spaces, defined by the building's two thick stone walls. Each space carries a unique atmosphere and materiality, tailored to its specific programme.

Block C

Block C is a long, double-height workshop space that spans the length of the building. Timber was chosen for quick construction, robustness and adaptability. The ceilings and high level walls are clad in low-fi acoustic rice panels, developed with Atelier LUMA and sourced from local rice fields. The stone walls are insulated with rice straw, creating deep external reveals for solar gain, and covered in a custom sunflower acoustic render. Lower walls are clad in a pressed sunflower panel, robust enough to handle electrical installations and easily replaceable. The two mezzanine staircases are clad in green sunflower panels.

Block B

Block B centres around a courtyard defined by white earth walls. Designed to enable isolated working without feeling segregated, it uses limited doors, relying on walls and corners for visual and acoustic division. White stone dust coming from the cutting waste of Sarragan Quarry in Baux-de-Provence is used in the earth walls to give them a unique light quality. Gravel from demolished buildings in Nîmes – brick, stone and ceramics – adds texture to the construction.

Block A

Distinct from the other two spaces, Block A is designed for large scale exhibitions, events and productions. The raw industrial aesthetic of the original building is preserved, with only the floor replaced, external walls insulated and roof repaired. The ceiling is left unpainted to highlight sections where water-damaged timbers were replaced. Two internal walls remain untouched, revealing various paint layers and finishes from its history.

Exterior

The building's facade was stripped back to stone and re-rendered with a lime plaster using broken tiles from the roof as aggregate for a textured finish. Large galvanised doors were added flush to the facade, maintaining vehicle access to the workshops. To reduce solar gain, south-facing windows were blocked, and an awning was added to the west facade to provide shade.

Garden

Le Magasin Électrique uses local micro-algae and helophyte plants to filter and recycle grey and yellow wastewater, which is directed to a garden that helps shelter and keep cool the southwest side of the building. The garden, designed on a grid with markers (like in a spreadsheet) for plant identification, contains tinctorial plants for dye experiments in the labs. The building also recycles rainwater for use in workshop sinks and toilets.

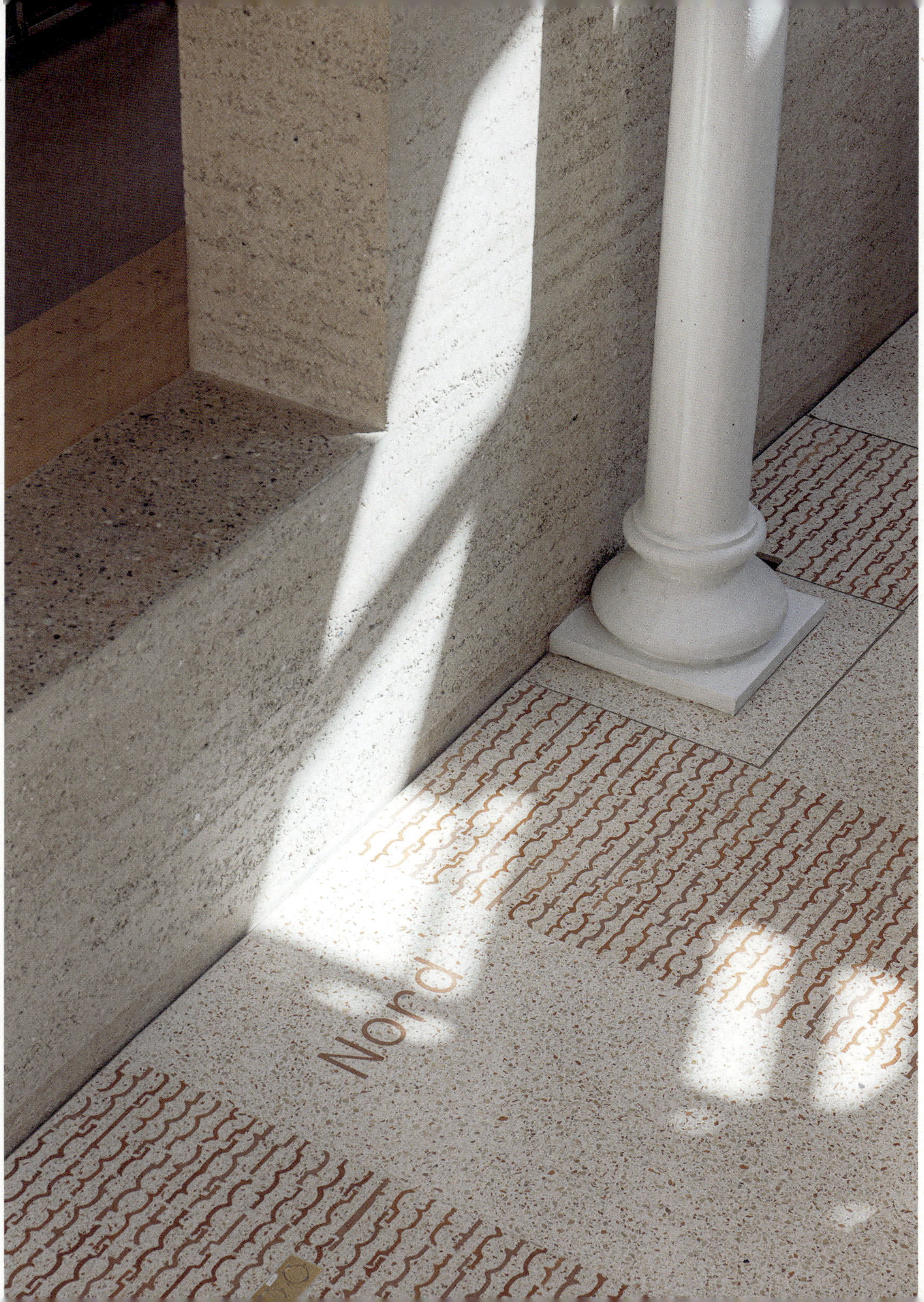
Nord

For centuries, the saltwater of the Rhône delta has been used to produce salt. Today, production is primarily destined for the agri-food and chemical industries. Since 2017, Atelier LUMA has been exploring the physical and aesthetic attributes of Camargue salt to develop materials that feature this local resource. This research opens up the salt industry to innovative applications in new fields, such as design and architecture.

One part of this activity involves in-depth research into the crystallisation process. When submerged in the salt marshes for several days, objects become covered in salt crystals, varying in size and colour depending on meteorological conditions. Another approach focusses on using moulding, pressing, heating and thermocompression to make three-dimensional prototypes.

In collaboration with local partners, the Crystallization Plant is exploring the natural crystallisation process in the salt marshes as a means of production. This process's low environmental impact makes it suitable for integration directly into the Camargue environment, in harmony with natural cycles and available resources.

Using custom frames, the Crystallization Plant has produced its first series of crystallized salt panel prototypes, suitable for architectural projects. The research into Camargue salt continues, expanding to study the raw material's intrinsic properties and possible new applications, such as energy production and light diffusion.

Door handle

At the bottom of the salt marshes, crystals naturally accumulate into blocks. These residues are shaped using tools designed for carving stone. Various forms for these frequently touched objects are used to explore salt's antibacterial properties.

Wall panels

Using custom anti-corrosion frames, a first series of crystallised salt panel prototypes has been produced using natural energy: salt crystallizes naturally on metal while immersed in the salt fields. 4,600 panels of crystallised salt cover the walls of the Tour LUMA in Arles after a collaboration extending from 2017 to 2021 between Frank Ghery, Atelier LUMA, Les Salins du Midi and designer Karlijn Sibbel.

Location
Camargue, France

Year
2017-2021

Sunflower Power develops bio-sourced materials in the bioregion, in keeping with the rhythms of the local sunflower industry. Sunflower cultivation in the Crau plains produces a large quantity of organic coproducts that are largely unused. After the oil is extracted, the protein-rich seeds are compressed into cakes, and the stems are left in the fields. Sunflower Power utilises these raw materials – the foamy structure of the stems, the exterior fibers and the dark green oil press cakes – to produce biomaterials.

The foamy stem marrow is combined with organic and mineral binders to produce composite materials with soundproofing properties. In partnership with laboratories, the properties of these composites were tested and validated. Wall panels made from this material, certified to meet architectural standards, were developed for the Magasin Électrique building as part of the "Building for Uncertainties" project. Additionally, the oil press cakes can be used to create bio-polymers, enabling the production of rigid mono-material objects through injection processes.

Further explored in the Bio Flash project, these experiments have also led to the development of flexible materials, such as vegan leather, produced using thermomechanical processes.

Panels
This material is composed of both marrow and bark. The marrow is a low-density, porous substance, similiar to polystyrene, with great acoustic properties. The bark is more like a hard, wood-like skin, rich in fibers and cellulose. The combination of these two materials using natural starch-based binders and mineral binders creates flame retardant panels that offer an effective solution for enhancing spatial acoustic absorption.

Press cake and applications
The Sunflower Press Cake, a co-product of oil extraction from seeds, is a biopolymer (protein) that behaves as a natural binder. This allows for the production of objects through heat-pressing, injection molding or extrusion. This biopolymer is used to make a leather-like soft material and objects, such as plant pots that biodegrade over time under outdoor conditions.

Location
The Crau plains, Provence, France

Sunflower leather and protein pastes

Location
Humlebæk, Denmark

Year
2024

Humlebæk biopolymer switches
The Humlebæk biopolymer switches aim to valorise natural Danish biopolymers found in various agricultural co-products, plants and macroalgae. The plugs are made entirely from biomass using the heat-pressing industrial method. Biopolymers such as alginate, cellulose and proteins act as binders through a plastification process, in which the raw material hardens under the simultaneous action of heat and pressure. Most of the time, the compressed biomass lacks sufficient waterproof qualities for this kind of application. Using 100% biomass switches would replace the ABS-injected plastics used normally for electronic components, offering a more sustainable version for the future.

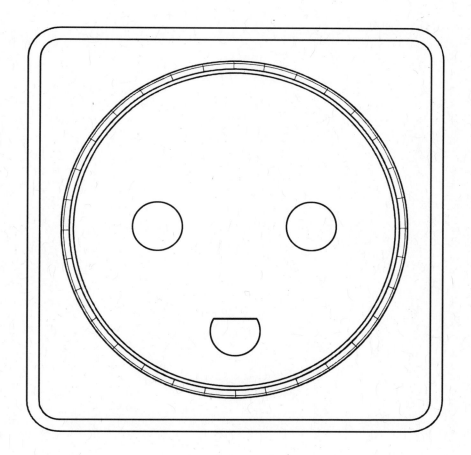

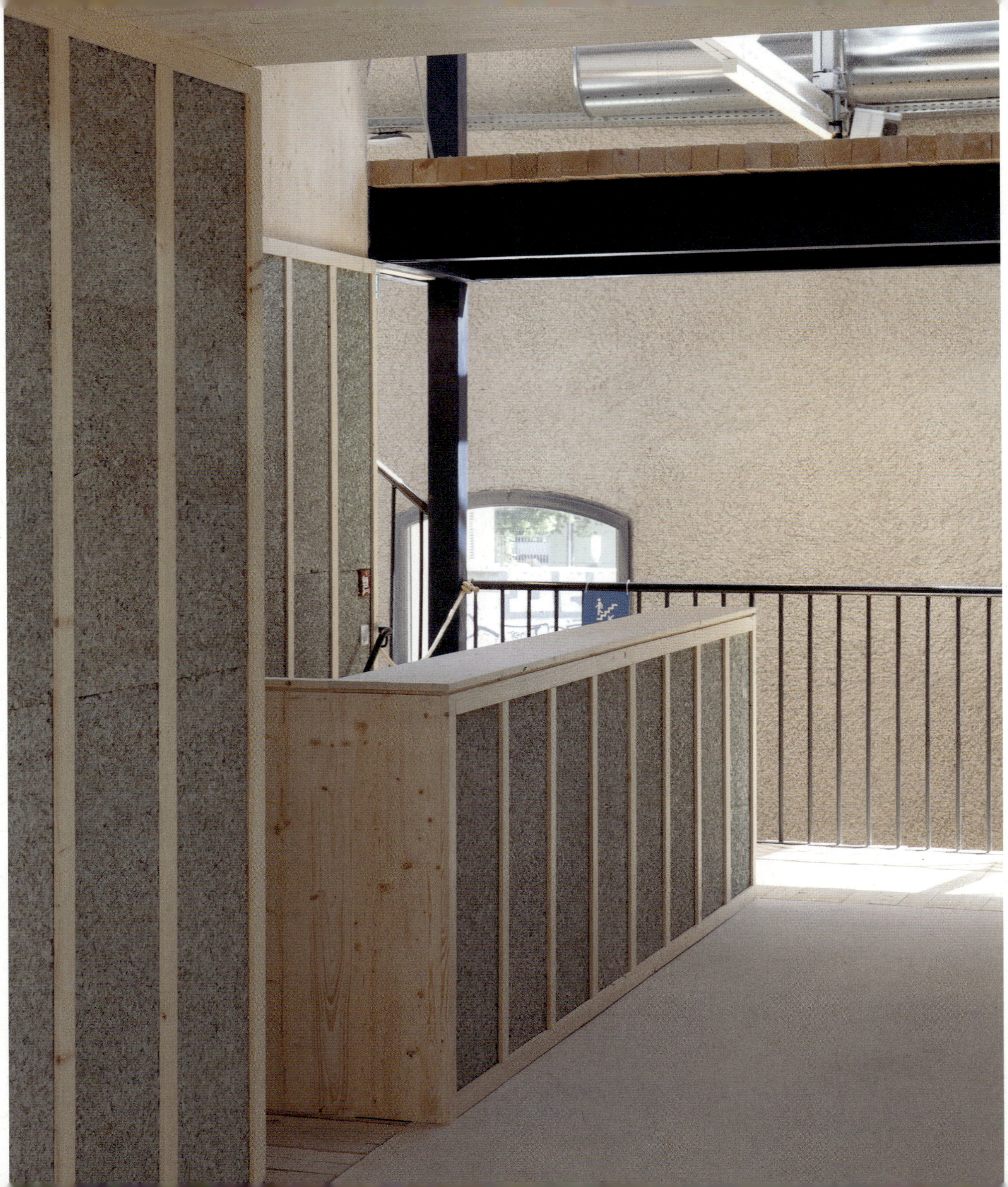

Sunflower wall panels

The Local Bio-Based Plastics project develops composite materials by integrating natural resources from the bioregion. It brings together designers, scientists and engineers to create bio-degradable, bio-sourced plastics, offering alternatives to fossil-based materials. This research aims to create various formulas, tailored for specific technical requirements like mechanical strength, fire resistance and water resistance, and suited for manufacturing processes such as injection moulding, extrusion, 3D printing and rotomoulding.

The team has identified abundant local resources like algae and undervalued by-products from agri-food industries, such as sunflower plants, olive pits and rice husks. These raw materials, in the form of powder or fibre, are mixed with bio-based plastic matrices and local pigments to enhance bioplastics.

Through the Biolab and the Bioplastics projects, local algae and fungi species are studied, including *Dunaliella salina, Arthrospira platensis, Halobacterium salinarum, Haematococcus, Gracilaria* and *Basidiomycota* fungi.

Rotational moulding is an industrial technique used to create large hollow objects at a relatively low cost. While typically associated with petroleum-based plastics, Atelier LUMA has studied this technique using bio-sourced and biodegradable plastic formulas. The team tested resources and raw materials commonly used in their labs and workshops, including algae, invasive plants and agricultural co-products. The first experimental object is small, spherical and versatile, allowing for easy unmoulding and adaption to various material properties. This object can be stacked and used as seating, lampshades, wastebaskets, flowerpots and more.

Location
Camargue, France, and Humlebæk, Denmark

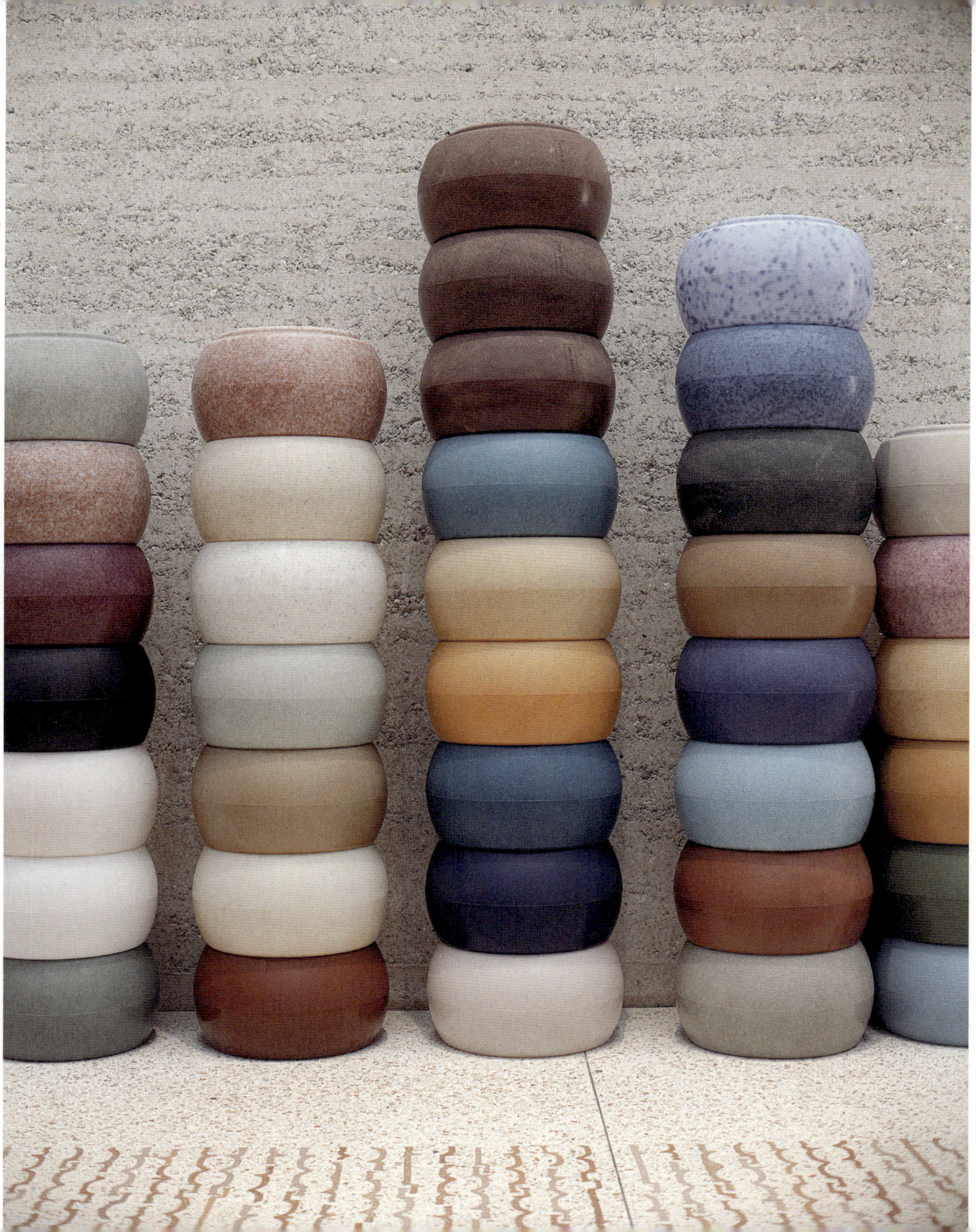

Humlebæk rotomouldings

The development of rotomoulded pieces was adapted to the Humlebæk region, employing a technique that allows for unique formulations for each object. This approach provides an excellent opportunity to test various locally available resources, including bioplastic matrices, fillers and pigments. Notable examples include the seaweeds harvested by Dansk Tang, beetroot by-products from sugar extraction, pigments extracted from *Ailanthus altissima* tree, blue pigment derived from woad (*Isatis tinctoria*) and pigments sourced from the chestnut tree. This development was made possible thanks to Plante-avlstationen v. Naturstyrelsen i Humlebæk.

Bioplastic 3D printing

The objects resulting from 3D printing research by Eric Klarenbeek and Maartje Dros during their residency at Atelier Luma include pieces that were partially scanned from archaeological artifacts from the Musée de l'Arles Antique, while others were original designs created by the designers.

Tiles

The algae-enhanced bioplastic was formed into tiles using an industrial injection process and tested for resistance to fire, UV exposure, water and cleaning products. It passed all tests, making it suitable for use as bathroom backsplash material. The tiles are available in 20 different colours, achieved using algae and dye plants. The restrooms in the LUMA Arles Tower are decorated with 30,000 of these small bioplastic tiles.

Antique dishes printed in 3D algae bioplastic and algea harvest in Camargue

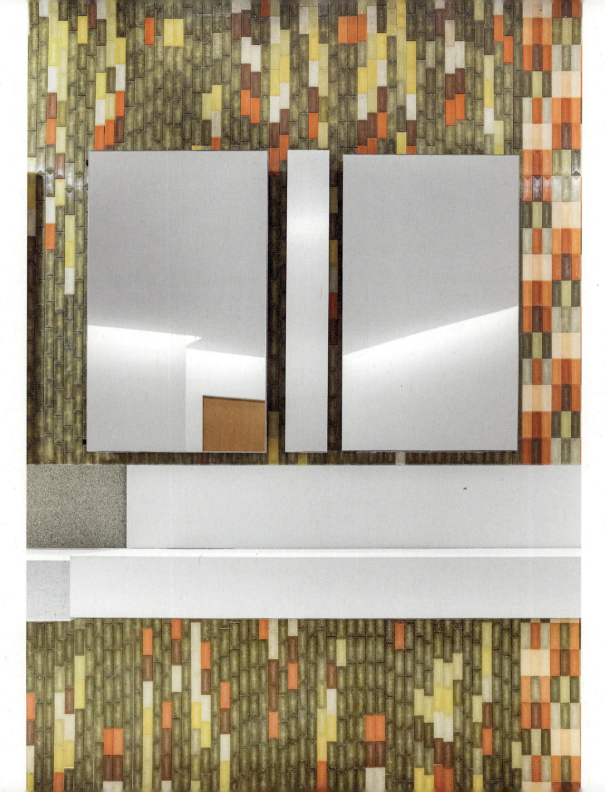

While some biologists consider invasive alien species a natural part of a landscape's evolution, most of the time these species pose significant challenges. Instead of simply destroying this biomass, Atelier LUMA reimagines invasive plants as renewable raw materials, creating new artisanal and industrial applications. For instance, leaves are used to extract dyes and paint, while larger trunks are peeled into veneers for fine objects like marquetry or industrial products like plywood. Other by-products, such as wood sticks with suckers, are repurposed into furniture and particle boards made from fine residual materials.

Ailanthus altissima (tree of heaven) is a common invasive plant found from Denmark to the Camargue. This pioneer species has many advantages for growth, such as its ability to thrive in narrow, highly polluted environments, including urban areas. It reproduces efficiently through seeds dispersed by wind and animals, as well as by suckering. When a tree is cut, the remaining roots respond to stress by producing more suckers, increasing its chances of survival. *Ailanthus altissima* grows rapidly, reaching heights of around 15 metres, and can live for approximately 50 years.

Ailanthus altissima chair

Denmark is also facing the problematic of several invasive plants, that threaten local biodiversity. *Ailanthus altissima* is one such species. With support from the engineering school at Les Arts et Métiers in Cluny, Atelier LUMA produces veneer from this plant, showcasing its potential for semi-industrial production. In collaboration with Danish Fritz Hansen, Atelier LUMA has used the veneer to create Arne Jacobsen's iconic 7 chair.

Dyed fabrics for scenography

The Color Geographies project explores local landscapes and the colours historically used in architecture, crafts and art within a specific bioregion. For this scenography, resources from Zeeland and the Camargue are combined to create a double bioregional colour palette featuring *Ailanthus altissima* and filamentous fungi extraction. Atelier LUMA paired this bright yellow colour with a deep purple from the Danish natural dye Sustainly.Red®. This fungi fermentation process gives a sustainable alternative to traditional colour extraction.

Location
Arles, France, and Humlebæk, Denmark

Year
2024

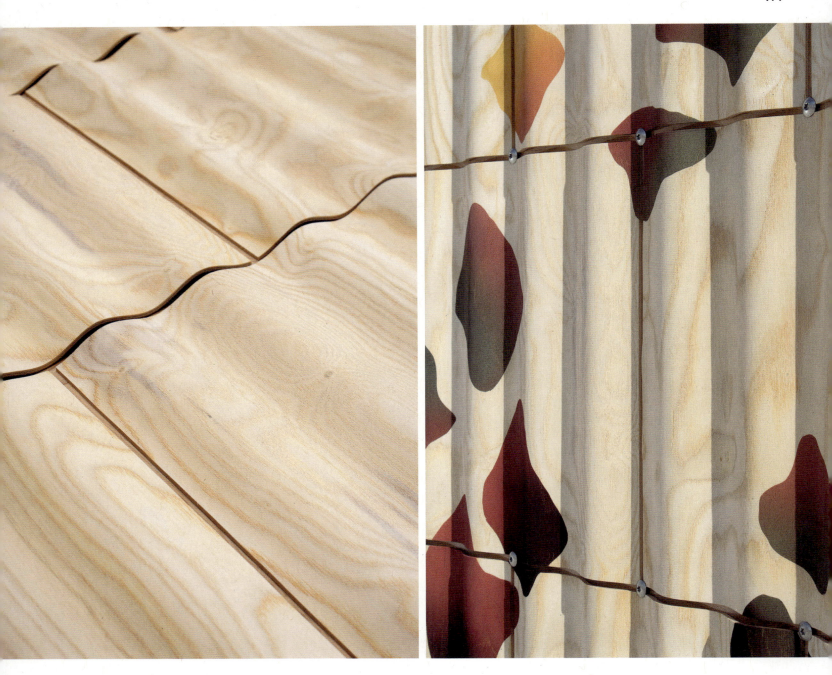

Arne Jacobsen's 7 chair produced by Fritz Hansen using Atelier LUMA's *Ailanthus Altissima* veneer

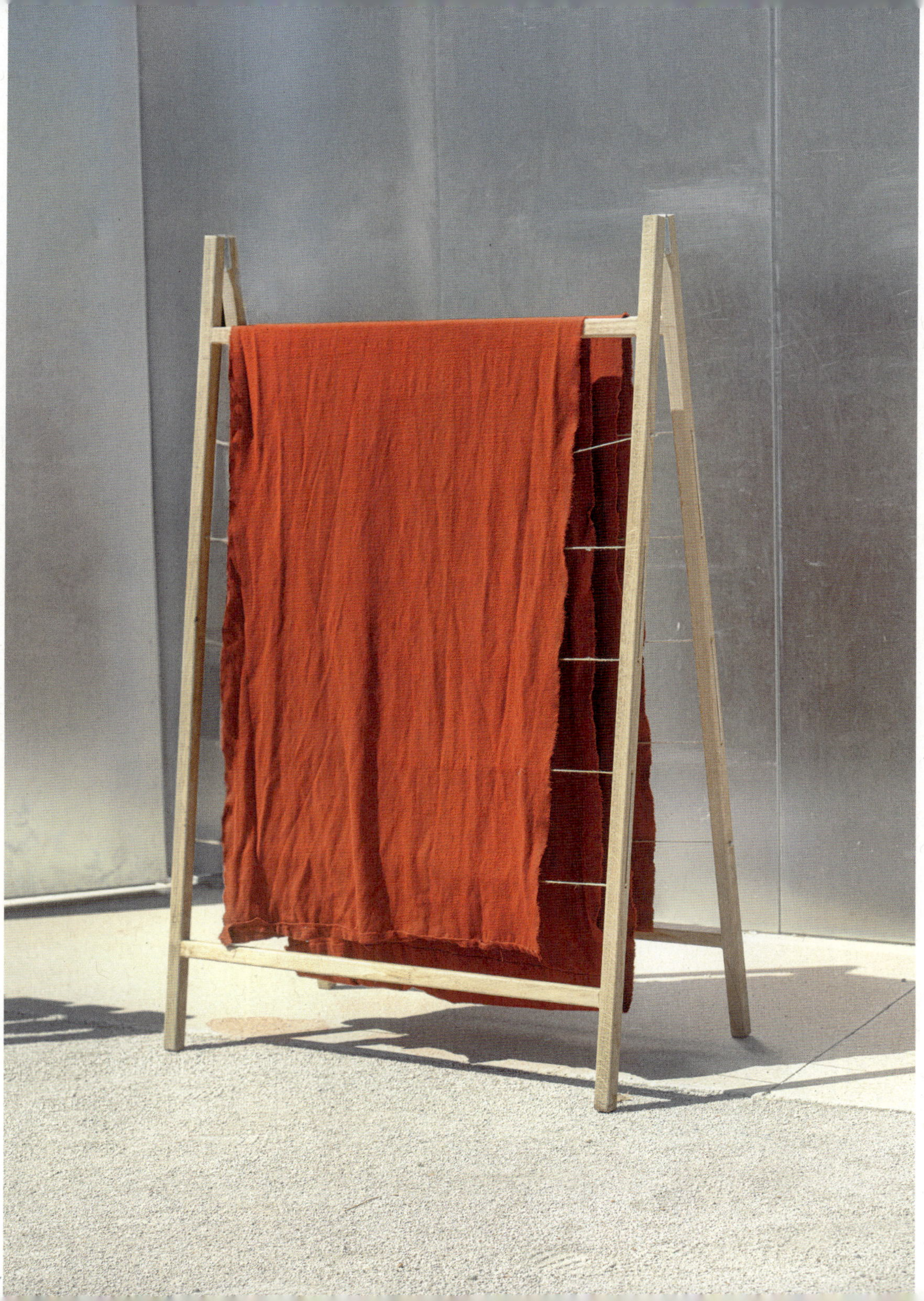

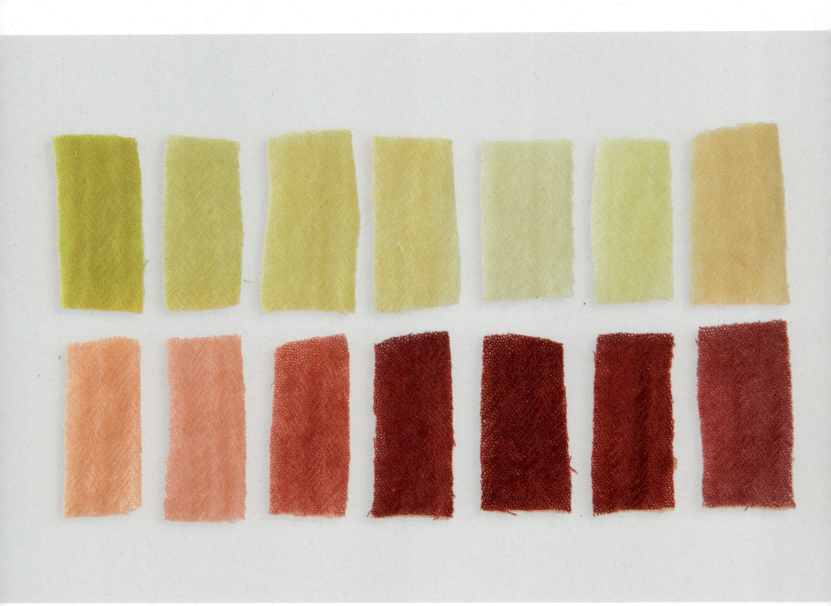

The Local Layer project started in 2021 during a workshop titled "Seaweed, the Lagoon and the City," hosted by the VAC Foundation in Venice and organized by Atelier LUMA in collaboration with Space Caviar. After a week of research, the team successfully 3D printed a brick made from fresh algae from the Venice lagoon and paper waste. The research continued at Atelier LUMA in Arles to develop a range of formulas using local agricultural co-products, algae binders, and paper pulp, aiming for higher mechanical resistance and lower deformation defects.

In 2024, the European project LINA offered the opportunity to collaborate with the Italian designer Anna Perugini on olive oil co-products. This became a series of bricks and a stool, demonstrating the strength of the material and its capacity to create larger pieces.

Humlebæk bricks

This brick reinterprets the classic brick and shows the range of shapes achievable through 3D printing, highlighting fluidity and interwoven forms. The colour palette, inspired by natural elements like stone, sand, and grass, contrasts with the earthy tones. The beige hue reflects the raw material, while the greens and grays are achieved by blending ochre into the mix. The Humlebæk formula includes paper pulp made from paper waste from the museum and Danish agricultural by-products.

Location
Italy, France and Denmark

Year
2021-2024

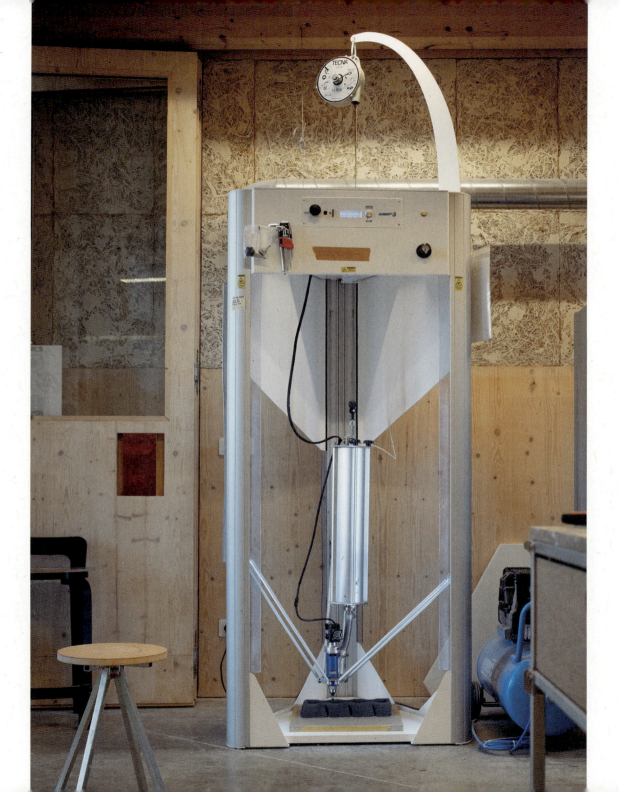

In collaboration with architects at Studio SOC, who explore connections between art, science and architecture, Atelier LUMA has developed a cartographic design and representation method to support its investigation and analysis of materials chains. This method can be applied to different bioregions to inventory and characterize the various players involved in a materials chain, as well as their connections, dependencies, and impacts. This cartographic tool aids design researchers in questioning the issues and challenges linked to a resource and its sector. The map not only visualizes and clarifies a complex territorial network, but also sparks strategic reflections that guide project development, exploring alternative and innovative development paths adapted to the bioregion. In the case of Humlebæk, Atelier LUMA analysed the reed and eelgrass industries to uncover their ecosystems in Denmark. This involved examining the nature of these raw material sources and the connected management policies, assets and threats, environmental impacts, social implications, knowledge-sharing, and preservation circuits.

Location
France and Denmark

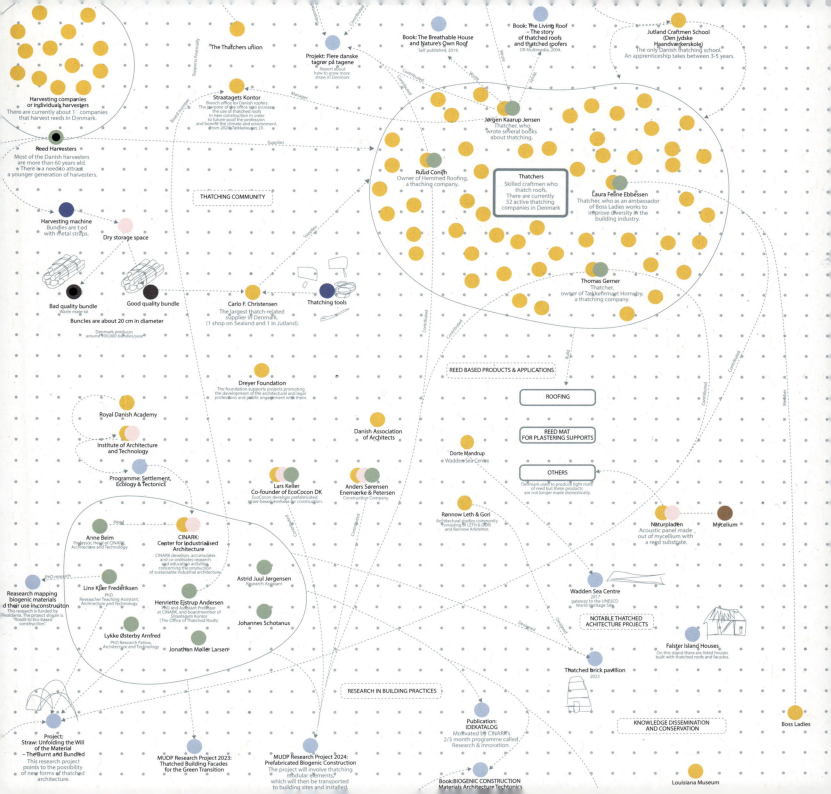

Harvesting companies or individuals harvesters
There are currently about 11 companies that harvest reeds in Denmark.

The Thatchers union

Projekt: Flere danske tagrør på tagene
Report about how to grow more straw in Denmark

Book: The Breathable House and Nature's Own Roof
Self published, 2019.

Book: The Living Roof – The story of thatched roofs and thatched roofers
DR Multimedia, 2004.

Jutland Craftmen School (Den Jydske Haandværkerskole)
The only Danish thatching school. An apprenticeship takes between 3-5 years.

Reed Harvesters
Most of the Danish harvesters are more than 60 years old. There is a need to attract a younger generation of harvesters.

Straatagets Kontor
Branch office for Danish roofers. The purpose of the office is to increase the use of thatched roofs in new construction in order to future-proof the profession and benefit the climate and environment. From 2024 Tækkelauget, DI.

Jørgen Kaarup Jensen
Thatcher, who wrote several books about thatching.

Supplies

THATCHING COMMUNITY

Harvesting machine
Bundles are tied with metal straps.

Dry storage space

Ruud Conijn
Owner of Hemmed Roofing, a thaching company.

Thatchers
Skilled craftmen who thatch roofs. There are currently 52 active thatching companies in Denmark.

Laura Feline Ebbessen
Thatcher, who as an ambassador of Boss Ladies works to improve diversity in the building industry.

Bad quality bundle
Waste material

Good quality bundle

Buncles are about 20 cm in diameter

Denmark produces around 400,000 bundles/year

Carlo F. Christensen
The largest thatch-related supplier in Denmark. (1 shop on Sealand and 1 in Jutland).

Thatching tools

Thomas Gerner
Thatcher, owner of Tækkefirmaet Hornæby, a thatching company.

REED BASED PRODUCTS & APPLICATIONS

Build

ROOFING

Dreyer Foundation
The foundation supports projects promoting the development of the architectural and legal professions and public engagement with them.

Royal Danish Academy

Danish Association of Architects

REED MAT FOR PLASTERING SUPPORTS

Institute of Architecture and Technology

Programme: Settlement, Ecology & Tectonics

Lars Keller
Co-founder of EcoCocon DK
EcoCocon develops prefabricated straw-based modules for construction.

Anders Sørensen
Enemærke & Petersen
Construction Company.

Dorte Mandrup
Wadden Sea Centre

OTHERS
Denmark used to produce light mats of reed but these products are not longer made domestically.

Rønnow Leth & Gori
Architectural studios community consisting of LETH & GORI and Rønnow Arkitekter.

Naturpladen
Acoustic panel made out of mycelium with a reed substrate.

Mycelium

Anne Beim
Professor, Head of CINARK, Architecture and Technology

CINARK: Center for Industrialised Architecture
CINARK develops, accumulates and co-ordinates research and education activities concerning the production of sustainable industrial architecture.

Astrid Juul Jørgensen
Research Assistant

Reasearch mapping biogenic materials and their use in construction
This research is funded by Realdania. The project slogan is "Roads to bio-based construction".

Line Kjær Frederiksen
PhD Researcher Teaching Assistant, Architecture and Technology

Henriette Ejstrup Andersen
PhD and Assistant Professor at CINARK, and boardmember of Straatagets Kontor (The Office of Thatched Roofs)

Johannes Schotanus

Wadden Sea Centre
2017 gateway to the UNESCO World Heritage Site.

NOTABLE THATCHED ACHITECTURE PROJECTS

Lykke Østerby Arnfred
PhD Research Fellow, Architecture and Technology

Jonathan Møller Larsen

Thatched brick pavillion
2023

Falster Island Houses
On this island there are listed houses built with thatched roofs and facades.

Project: Straw: Unfolding the Will of the Material – The Burnt and Bundled
This research project points to the possibility of new forms of thatched architecture.

RESEARCH IN BUILDING PRACTICES

Publication: IDEKATALOG
Motivated by CINARK's 2/3 month programme called, Research & Innovation.

KNOWLEDGE DISSEMINATION AND CONSERVATION

Boss Ladies

MUDP Research Project 2023: Thatched Building Facades for the Green Transition

MUDP Research Project 2024: Prefabricated Biogenic Construction
The project will involve thatching modular elements, which will then be transported to building sites and installed.

Book: BIOGENIC CONSTRUCTION
Materials Architecture Techtonics

Louisiana Museum

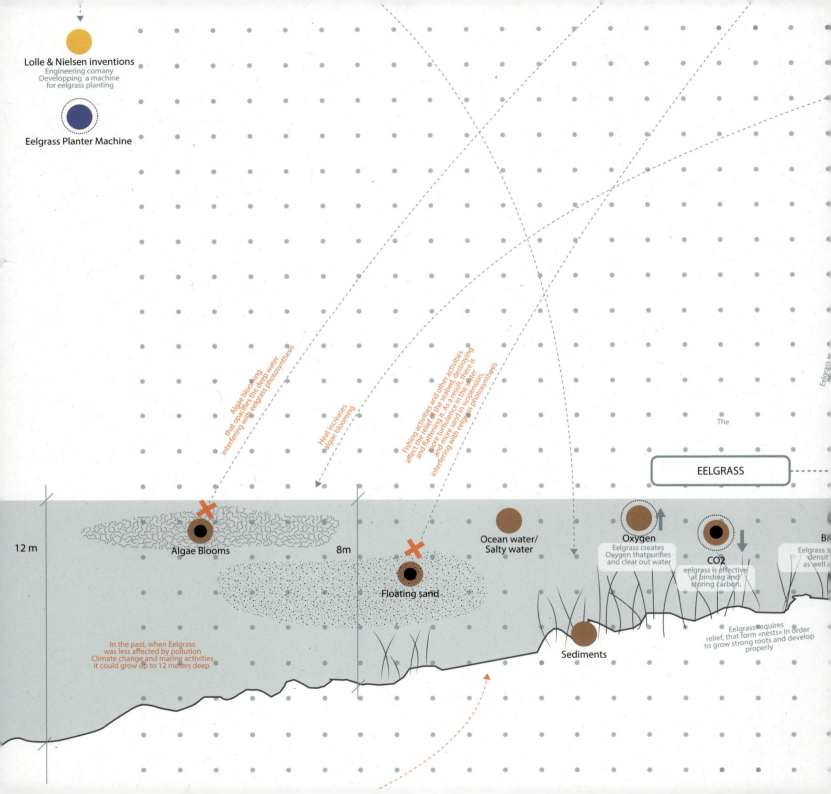

Lolle & Nielsen inventions
Engineering comany
Developping a machine
for eelgrass planting

Eelgrass Planter Machine

Algae blooming
that opacifies the deep water
interfering with eelgrass photosynthesis

Heat increases
algae blooming

Fishing activities and other activities
affect the relief the seabed, destroying
and flattening it. As a result, destroying
more turbulence in the water, there is
interfering with eelgrass photosynthesis

EELGRASS

12 m

Algae Blooms

8m

Floating sand

Ocean water/
Salty water

Oxygen
Eelgrass creates
Oxygen thatpurifies
and clear out water

CO2
eelgrass is effective
at binding and
storing carbon.

Bi
Eelgrass s
densit
as well a

In the past, when Eelgrass
was less affected by pollution
Climate change and marine activities
it could grow up to 12 meters deep

Sediments

Eelgrass requires
relief, that form «nests» in order
to grow strong roots and develop
properly

The

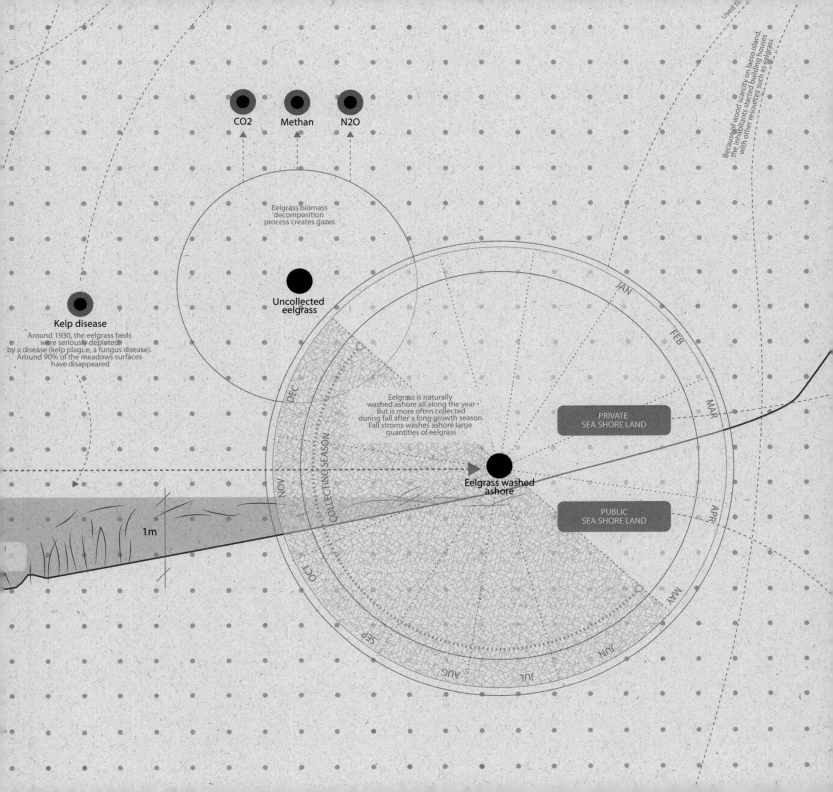

CO2   Methan   N2O

Eelgrass biomass
decomposition
process creates gazes

Uncollected
eelgrass

Kelp disease
Around 1930, the eelgrass beds
were seriously depleted
by a disease (kelp plague, a fungus disease).
Around 90% of the meadows surfaces
have disappeared

Eelgrass is naturally
washed ashore all along the year
But is more often collected
during fall after a long growth season.
Fall stroms washes ashore large
quantities of eelgrass

PRIVATE
SEA SHORE LAND

PUBLIC
SEA SHORE LAND

Eelgrass washed
ashore

1m

JAN
FEB
MAR
APR
MAY
JUN
JUL
AUG
SEP
OCT
NOV
DEC

COLLECTING SEASON

Because of wood scarcity on Iaeso Island,
the inhabitants started building houses
with other resources such as eelgrass

METTE RAMSGAARD THOMSEN
Thank you Jenny for the great opportunity of this discussion. The exhibition is such an exciting place to share the breadth of your practice. Your visionary work with bio-manufacturing, programmable matter, textiles and bio-mimicry shows the frontiers of how architecture can be designed and built. What I find exciting is the opportunity to bring these ideas together, how they as a collection construct a new architectural domain.

How do you think of your practice and how it engages novel design strategies and manufacturing technologies, and more broadly how does it develop new discourse on what architecture can be. What kind of liaisons do you find emerging?

JENNY SABIN
Thank you, Mette. In looking back upon the last 20 years or so of my transdisciplinary collaborative work, I would say there are three distinct phases where liaisons emerge. Of course, there are overlaps, and it's certainly not linear but very much a process. The first phase of my collaborative work focusses on *learning from nature* and learning specifically from cell and biological systems to produce ecological design models and material analogues for reciprocal and bio-informed processes and thinking in design. This includes liaisons with cell and molecular biologists, engineers and material scientists. The second phase focusses on *mimicking nature* or the transfer of material and geometric properties and characteristics present in natural systems such as the wings of the blue morpho butterfly into new responsive material systems that are scalable for architecture. For example, my early collaborative project, eSkin, focussed on the topic of structural colour in nature and the development of responsive skins for buildings. PolyForm incorporated this fundamental research in an immersive permanent public pavilion on Cornell's campus. This entailed cutting across length scales for new opportunities in programmable matter and exploring responsive and adaptive materials by design. More recently, what has emerged through this robust foundation is a more mature phase of *collaborating with nature*.

This work focusses both on biodesign and biomanufacturing, working in collaboration with natural systems to open up new opportunities in the context of sustainability with living materials that are adaptive and cyclically engaged with their environments. This affords new opportunities to shift away from, for example, materials made from petrochemicals to biopolymers. Within this third stage of work, we collaborate with biological and environmental engineers and other colleagues in chemical and biomolecular engineering to design new living materials and to explore biomanufacturing opportunities.

MRT

It seems to me that the central remit is about moving from a tradition which defines materials through an essentially geometric domain to a much more performative understanding of materials. During the last 15 years, computational design has been examining how these performances could be formalised and computed. But your work takes many of these questions further. By looking at new material classes such as nano technology and new fabrication systems such as biotechnology, you are asking how these systems and the materials themselves can be engineered. How do you think about design agency with these materials? How do you engage designerly outcomes with these advanced material classes that you are developing?

JS

Maybe I can address this question with an example of our efforts in putting DNA to work, in which we design and engineer specific DNA strands. In this work, material agency is steered towards particular performances and biochemical interactions with the local environment. This work builds on our multiple years of work with digitally fabricated ceramics, bricks, bio-tiles, Polytiles, Polybricks and is a multiyear collaborative project with my colleague, Dan Luo, who is in biological and environmental engineering at Cornell.

In these recent experiments, this mode of bio-informed thinking has expanded to designing with actual life through DNA-steered ceramic materials, and also living glazes that feature dynamic feedback mechanisms. So, in this way, agency also arises from a dynamic reciprocity with the local environment to reflect upon new questions and opportunities for adaptive and living materials through advanced processes and additive manufacturing, but also, importantly, coupled with DNA hydrogel development.

And in the first phase, we have primarily focussed on programmable bio-functionalities and controlling the emission of cell-free light. We're developing these living glazes with DNA that are cell-free. In this case, DNA, which is the information storage molecule for biological systems, has been a known material for engineering for quite some time.

But there aren't so many applications at the architectural scale. And so, we've been able to work with specific sequences focussed on luciferase, the magical firefly. So, we are working with input energy and output energy, and the result is light.

Imagine a wall that features these living glazes on 3D printed tiles or bricks that can not only alert you to local contaminants in the environment through the emission of light, but also, through biochemical interactions, actually cleanse the local environment of certain contaminants.

MRT

That's so interesting. In CITA, we've just started an interdisciplinary collaboration with marine biology. We're looking at cyanobacteria and how they change colour with different levels of CO_2. Our aim is to use them as a signalling organism to reveal if there are high levels of CO_2 in an environment.

Working with living organisms fundamentally challenges architectural design methods. Instead of thinking through a static design space we need to question how ideas of lived time, propagation, nutrition and environment expand our design language. I think it's very interesting, how are you working with these ideas?

JS

Yes, so the ceramic portion that is 3D printed, they're fired. And sometimes, we selectively include other types of glazes so that we can steer exactly where the DNA hydrogels will adhere to the ceramic surfaces. So, the DNA hydrogels are not fired. That wouldn't work at all. They would cease to function. The ceramic piece, the clay itself, is printed and then fired and chemically changed to the ceramic. In recent collaborative work, we have developed living glazes with engineered DNA from baker's yeast to metabolize formaldehyde. This has raised questions about life-cycle nutrients for the living glaze and about the agency of the living material.

MRT

This is such a poetic way to rethink what glazing can be. I think our field is in a period of great development right now. We both have backgrounds in computational design. While the methodologies and technological platforms have matured, there is simultaneously a search for how to deploy these methods in a climate crisis.

In our work this has led to a focus on circularity and biogenic materials. In many ways, circular design can be criticised as slightly mechanistic, and its infrastructure is also quite deterministic. I think there is opportunity for our field to reframe the idea of circularity around a new set of material classes that have different ways of self-transforming into other material classes. This makes bio-based materials and biotechnology so interesting as a novel place to reconsider architecture.

How do you frame the material vision of your work?

JS

Yes, so this exhibition is focussed on drawing links between research and practice, and in my case, linking what I do collaboratively and in the sciences and engineering with how that's moved into the built environment. Sometimes there are clear and direct links between the ongoing fundamental research in my lab and how that is transformed and applied to built projects.

But the arc and timing is variable, also in terms of how the work is conducted. The cadence in the lab, in terms of the pace and depth of inquiry is much, much slower compared to the day-to-day work of my practice. They're separate teams. They're funded completely differently and exist in separate spaces.

For example, in my lab at Cornell, we may have four to seven years of funding to collaboratively examine, say, kirigami geometry, structural colour, or the roles of mechanics and the environment, in specifying changes in growth and morphogenesis in diverse biological systems. These deep and rigorous investigations give rise to new design drivers for adaptive and responsive materials and architectural assemblies. Whereas, in the practice, we operate at a much faster pace where site conditions, programme, diverse communities and scale inform the projects.

Not all the work that we're engaged in, in terms of the fundamental research, is ready to be scaled. So, we find alternative material systems where we can explore behaviours and concepts and specific performances that we're steering, in the context of the research, towards applied urban-scale public projects.

One specific example would be our work on the dynamics of light and energy, looking at structural colour, how we can transfer specific patterns and geometries from a nanoscale into an architectural scale. Here we work with photoluminescence and solar-active fibres as a way of pushing that opportunity, in terms of interactivity happening with diverse publics, as opposed to within the confines of the lab. And increasingly, we're getting more permanent commissions, large urban-scale projects. For me, success comes from how the projects occasion diverse engagements, not just with people, but with multiple species in these urban settings.

That takes time. One of the productive hurdles that we've had to navigate, or that I've had to navigate as an architectural designer working with scientists and engineers, is that most of my collaborators engage in fundamental research. It's not that they're not interested in application. They just don't do that. It's not a part of their work. So, I am frequently in the position of pushing the team to think about scalability and how we can begin to coordinate and choreograph all of these dynamic parameters, to form a plan and consider how it can be applied and materialised.

MRT

I always felt that, in collaborating across disciplines, the point is to understand each other's goals. You have to understand what the cutting edge is in the different fields. How you can combine the goals of those fields into novel strategies.

JS

Yes, it's interesting because the pursuit of communicating these dynamic material conditions also brings up the topic of visualisation and modelling. From the very beginning, I was surprised by what wasn't happening in my scientific colleagues' labs, in terms of how they were visualizing, for example, cellular data.

I immediately saw an opportunity for my team and I to contribute, both technologically, but also in terms of the relevance of design and synthetic thinking in science. And so, being able to represent and spatialise and materialise these data in a new way has been incredibly impactful.

In trying to model what we're seeing, a whole new conversation opens up that's about the collaborative work, in terms of what the scientists are used to seeing and how they represent and diagram and notate certain behaviours, and how we, as designers, go about that.

MRT

I assume that there are multiple models of exchange between your lab and your practice. I am also curious about their audiences, the different recipients of your work, and therefore the very different models of experience that you offer. How do you think about this in your design?

JS

I would say it manifests in a couple of different ways. One is simply through the nature of the work. For example, with Lumen, which is probably, to date, our largest digitally knit interactive public canopy project that we developed as part of the Young Architects programme for MoMA and MoMA PS1. At that point, I had over a decade of experience working with knit material systems that incorporate high-tech, responsive fibres and I felt confident that the material system was ready to be pushed, literally, to go outdoors and to engage with large numbers of people and diverse communities.

It featured two large integrated canopy systems, three 42 ft tensegrity towers, and the entire project was designed to be dynamic – to not only respond to the changing conditions of light and the environment, but also to the various programmes that took place throughout the week. We also had to consider rainfall and the fine-scale programming of how the knit canopy system would respond to large amounts of rain during the hot, humid summer months in New York City.

I had people come up to me and say, "I wish this project was in my child's playground", or, "I come here on Saturdays to enjoy the music and art events, and then I come here during the week to eat my lunch. I feel calm." Or some people said, "I wish this was in our local hospital." So, there's something about the work that's informed by years of deep inquiry into morphogenesis and multicellular structures that's not literally translated.

But the thinking is translated, as a way of working systemically, that produces architectures that are fuzzy, that don't have hard boundaries or finite edges, that inspire moments of pause and wonder, of gathering. And then, at the same time, these open new ways of thinking about space and co-produced materialities that we can contribute to in public spaces. Years of rigorous inquiry into biological systems, developing ecological thinking models, mimicking and collaborating with nature, I think, has produced possibilities within an architecture that is never quite complete until it's engaged with by humans and other species. There's a potential for not only empathy, but also for the architecture to evolve over time.

MRT

I'm reminded of a beautiful project you did in collaboration with the biologist Peter Lloyd Jones at the Sabin+Jones LabStudio, the Branching Morphogenesis project. In that project, you were examining material organisation and how to represent complex material order. It was a clear way to express how interdisciplinary work might lead to a different idea of what materials are, how they perform and are structured and at the same time bring in architecturally specific concerns of representation as a means to understand this material makeup, so that we can gain insight, and perhaps also control, over these material systems.

I remember this clearly, because we were working on textile systems in the same period. For me this idea that textiles can act as a model, as well as a material for architecture is really fundamental. I think that textiles are a helpful way of trying to understand what's at stake in digital design, because by being able to control or understand the material connectivity, we become able to understand the methods of fabrication.

How do you see this project now, almost 20 years later?

JS

I think, Mette, this is where we share a number of synergies and overlaps in our exploration of knit and textiles as a potent material ground for exploring how dynamic processes and biology can, in an analogous way, integrate with the knit, from stitch to stitch, to much larger variegated swaths. As you say, it's both a model and a way of steering materiality, where the design process is informed by systems and relationships and dynamic processes and the elusive complexity of the knit that affords unexpected and emergent conditions that can then be steered and computed further.

And so, Branching Morphogenesis was very much situated in that kind of collaborative thinking space. We were modelling endothelial cellular networks that form the vascular lining of the human lung, and we were looking at the role of environment in specifying changes in geometry, materiality, pattern and history, etc., as a set of dynamic feedback loops or reciprocal relationships between environment and form.

Could we take the visualisations that we were developing of the data, the spatial modelling, and make them material? And, yes, it's an abstraction. Each loop, or, in later projects, if we're working with knit, each stitch, each dropped stitch, each hole, contains information. That coupling of what comes from biology with material parameters can produce really powerful results.

We continue to develop tools and models for visualising and spatially coordinating and modelling dynamic cellular structures and some of those tools are brought into the realm of prototyping.

And that forces, I think, a shift where we begin to think about what is actually scalable, versus when there is a need to shift to a different material system.

And then some of those successful prototypes are brought into the realm of architecture and ecological re-considerations of what architecture can be in the built environment. That's where my practice comes in. It's very much a process.

MRT

This idea of ecology is really interesting. It's also within the remit of the exhibition, how architecture can respond to changing climate needs. Sometimes architects are asked to respond to sustainability in an imposed fashion, where the goals and solutions are ideated outside of our domain. But we do not only respond to ecology, we participate in it. How can architecture perform as part of an ecology, and actively use design as a means to bring different measures together and balance them? This is a new vision of architectural practice.

JS

Yes, my recent work is more so focussed on collaborating directly with nature and biological systems, at least within the lab, and this has resulted in 1:1 scale building products.

These tiles and bricks incorporate biodesign and biomanufacturing. We work with living organisms to produce biomolecules with potential applications in architecture or agriculture, even medicine in some cases. Which is, I think, a new model for how we may approach the problem of sustainability and climate change, where we shift away from a paradigm that's focussed on resource consumption and energy-intensive manufacturing processes that require petrochemicals and oil drilling and extraction processes that have fundamentally contributed to the situation that we're in now, to one that looks at the promise of biopolymers and embedded circular bio-micro factories. Some of the products that are man-ufactured with these petrochemicals, which are horrific for the environment, which produce formaldehyde, for example, are unfortunately still plentiful in our built environments.

Multiple new high-rise apartment buildings feature high concentrations of formaldehyde. And so, we're working collaboratively on these bio-tiles, where we're simply working with programmable, yeast-based living materials, where the chemical and bimolecular engineers on the team are designing and engineering the yeast to metabolise the formaldehyde and clean the local environment. These bio-tiles with living glazes have the potential to create self-healing conditions by breaking down toxic chemicals in our indoor environments.

Doing that work and opening up this new paradigm, this allows for a new model for how we might approach the problem of sustainability through direct collaboration with these biological systems. And also, it points to a shift away from a focus on resource consumption to a focus on renewal and self-healing and a kind of deep ecology that can be developed in concert with these natural systems.

MRT

I'm reminded of Jorge Otero-Pailos' seminal article, "The Ambivalence of Smoke," in which he discusses the emergence of white glazed terracotta in the late 19th century and how it was a response to an environmental crisis in the form of pollution. This new wonder material was inherently self-cleaning in that with every rainfall the building would wash off its dirt and grime and stand anew. The article asks profound questions, such as: what does architecture want to be? What does it mean, the performance of the architectural surface that we dress our buildings in? How do we think about ageing in our built environment and where does this idea of eternal novelty come from?

When I was at university, architecture was fundamentally a social construct. We were taught very, very little about materials and a lot about programme. I think the next generation, that we are part of forming through our teaching practices, is much more informed and interested in directly engaging with materiality. This leads to new questions – what kind of material should architecture be made of, and what should we ask of our materials and how does architecture itself change once we have a completely different sensitivity to what materials can and should do?

JS

Yes, and I think this also points to what I was talking about, in terms of the built work in my practice and how people respond to it, how they describe it. How they describe their engagement, their experiences, the impact the work has on them, that there's the potential for the architecture to evolve and change through people's direct engagement with it.

And this next level, which I would say is a complete paradigm shift, in terms of how we think of manufacturing, is a shift towards the biomanufacturing of real dynamic feedback loops between the environment and the biology and the host, or the architectural surface, which facilitates and contributes to a kind of continuously regenerative ecology and materiality.

Unlike the terracotta white-glazed surface architecture that you described, which is complete in a way, what we're talking about here is the possibility of something that truly evolves, that's biosynthetic, that it's not just responsive but truly adaptive. There's the potential for those fuzzy spatial edges to continue to expand and materialise. And that, to me, is very exciting as a way of considering how the built work can continue to engage and interact with community, but also contribute to other biological performances.

MRT

If we return to your description of the exhibition design, there is a sense of wanting to navigate or structure a sort of evolution of thinking. You seem to constantly be asking: How can architecture engage in profound conversations with a wide range of specializations, beyond specific interdisciplinary collaborations?

Your contribution is, of course, to gather people from very different fields. Both in your practice and your academic career you have constructed a radical new vision. Through this you encourage questions like: what kind of architecture can these new interdisciplinary concerns produce? How will it be to experience an architecture of a completely different materiality, as subjects or inhabitants of a space with completely different definitions of architectural axioms of boundary, ground and temporality? I think these are essential parts of the architectural project, to keep questioning the body of architecture. This is an aesthetic concern, but perhaps even more so a deep probing of the designerly poetics that architecture embodies.

JS

It's beautiful, and I think we also have a responsibility and obligation to communicate what it is that we're doing in the lab, to general audiences, to communities that may not encounter this type of work in their daily lives or in their own work.

A big part of the practice that excites me and drives the work is that communication. What matters is that moment of inspiration, of sheer wonder, of: where did this come from? What is behind this? Why does it look that way? And why do I feel this way when I interact with this new type of space? That is so powerful, and is, I would say, probably the biggest reason why I have my practice. Many people say, "Oh, Jenny, you could just have your lab and the teaching", and sure, that is a huge part of what I do.

At the end of the day, I think the biggest impact that I make is through my teaching and getting students to think just a little differently about how they're approaching design and the process of design and materialising what they're working on and to understand how to collaborate and communicate across disciplines.

But for me, the practice is really where we can communicate and make an impact in a deep societal way. Whether that means inspiring new approaches to the problem of sustainability and climate change through special materials that are not only performative and functional but also deeply aesthetic and beautiful, or innovating new forms of public space through biosynthetic design processes, my practice is where the transdisciplinary research is really tested and applied.

The work with responsive textile materials builds upon the ongoing work in the Jenny Sabin Lab (JSLab) at Cornell University on biological cellular surface design, structural colour and designing with light. In nearly every project featuring digitally knit surface structures, the knit materials include two high-tech responsive yarns and a white fire-retardant synthetic 'fill' yarn. The photoluminescent fibres emit light after the absorption of photons (electromagnetic radiation) from the sun or UV lights. The photons within the fibre are excited and then relax, causing the glowing effect across the fabric structures. The solar-active threads change colour in the presence of the sun or UV. The fibres undergo molecular excitation transition where the molecules in the presence of the sun shift into a range within the electromagnetic spectrum that is visible to the human eye. At a molecular scale, small crystals within the fibre reveal their colours in the presence of a UV light source.

Commencing with the myThread Pavilion for Nike Inc. in 2012 and recently Purl for IMKAN in Abu Dhabi and exoKnit for Neuehouse in New York City, Jenny Sabin Studio (JSS) collaborates with industry partners and manufacturers to innovate large-scale applications of digitally knit surface architectures. Having worked with Shima Seiki and their WHOLEGARMENT© technology for over 10 years, a streamlined process for knit production ensures accuracy of each 3D seamlessly knitted component part and efficient fabrication planning.

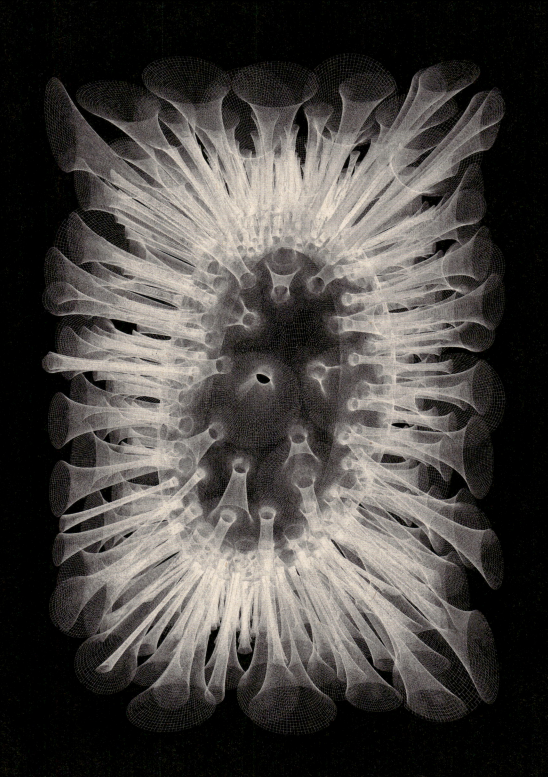

By night, Lumen is knitted light, bathing visitors in a responsive glow of photoluminescence; by day, it offers succour from the summer heat, immersing participants in delicious ground clouds of cooling mist. Lumen is a socially and environmentally responsive structure that adapts to the presence of bodies, heat and sunlight. A lightweight knitted fabric of responsive tubular structures, combined with canopies of cellular components, employs recycled textiles along with photoluminescent and solar-active yarns that absorb, collect and deliver light.

This environment offers spaces of respite, exchange and engagement. A misting system responds to visitors' proximity, activating fabric stalactites that produce a refreshing micro-climate. Lumen is an open lightweight, high-performing, formfitting and adaptive architecture. Held in tension within the PS1 courtyard matrix of walls, Lumen applies insights and theories from biology, materials science, mathematics and engineering. The project is mathematically generated through form-finding simulations informed by the sun, site, materials, programme, and the structural morphology of knitted cellular components. Knitting and textile fabrication offer a material ground for exploring these nonstandard fibrous potentials. As with cell networks, materials find their own form where the flow of tension forces through both geometry and matter serve as active design parameters. Resisting a biomimetic approach, Lumen employs an analogic design process where complex material behaviour and processes are integrated with personal engagement and diverse programmes. Through direct references to the flexibility and sensitivity of the human body, Lumen integrates adaptive materials and architecture where code, pattern, human interaction, environment, geometry and matter operate together as a conceptual design space.

Lumen was the winning proposal for the 2017 YAP, annual competition hosted by MoMA and MoMA PS1 from 1998-2019.

Client
Museum of Modern Art and MoMA PS1,
Young Architects Program (YAP) 2017

Location
MoMA PS1, Queens, NY, USA

Year
2017

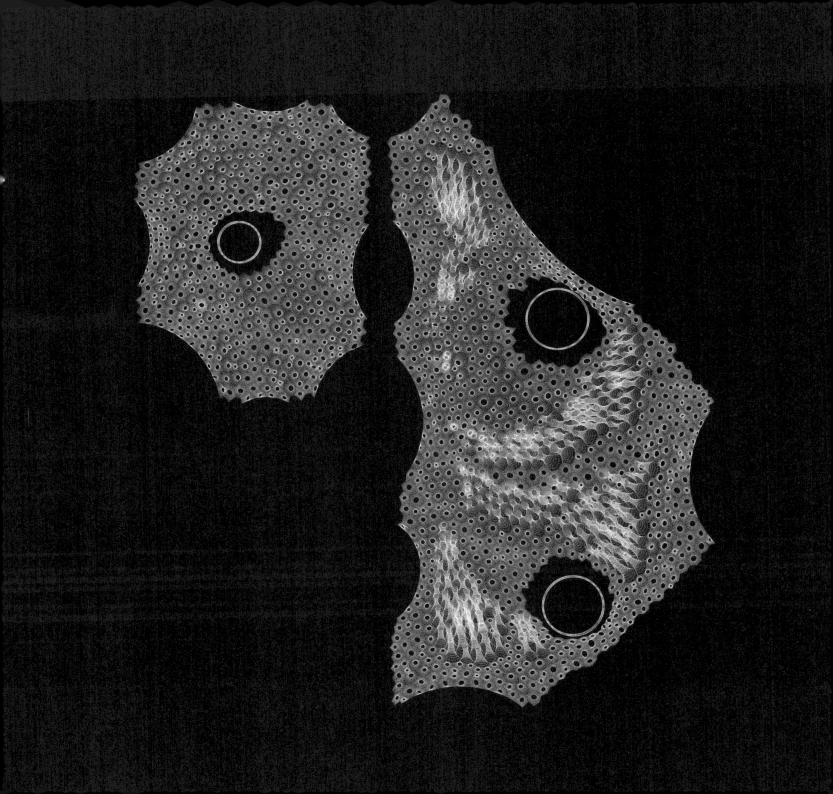

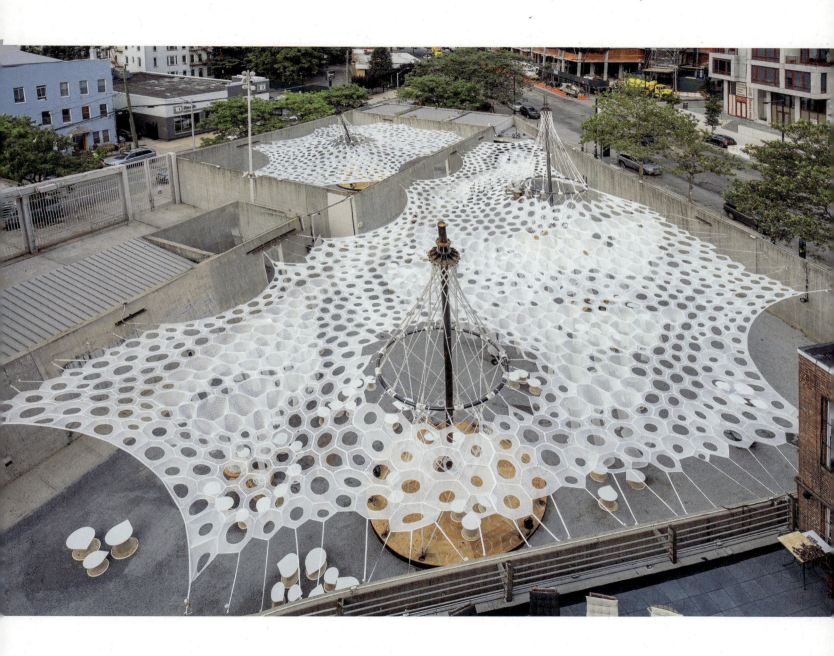

Mathematically generated and inspired by cellular networks, Poly-Thread is a freestanding inhabitable form. The digitally knitted fabric structure is held in tension with integrated fibreglass tubing. Working analogically and digitally, physical knit fabric prototypes and minimal surface relaxation models operate together as a materially directed generative design process.

Models borrowed from architects – such as tensegrity structures and geodesic domes – have led to radical new insights into how living systems, such as cells, tissues and whole organisms, are assembled and function, as well as to a new understanding of how the micro-ecology of cells influences the genome. Similarly, models borrowed from biology, particularly regarding self-organization, metadata structures and the emergence of complex, non-linear global systems from simple local rules of organization, have led to radical new forms and structural organizations in architectural design. The design process for PolyThread explored the architectural potential of these emergent cellular surface morphologies to promote engaging interactions between visitors and experimental responsive architecture. PolyThread employs photoluminescent and solar active yarns that absorb and deliver light. Portable and lightweight, such a structure could be used outdoors to absorb light from the sun during the day and release it at night. Material responses to light as well as human participation were integral parts of our exploratory approach to the subjects of beauty and adaptive architecture. PolyThread was originally on view as part of the 5th Cooper Hewitt Design Triennial: *Beauty*.

Client
Cooper Hewitt Smithsonian Design Museum

Location
New York, USA

Year
2016

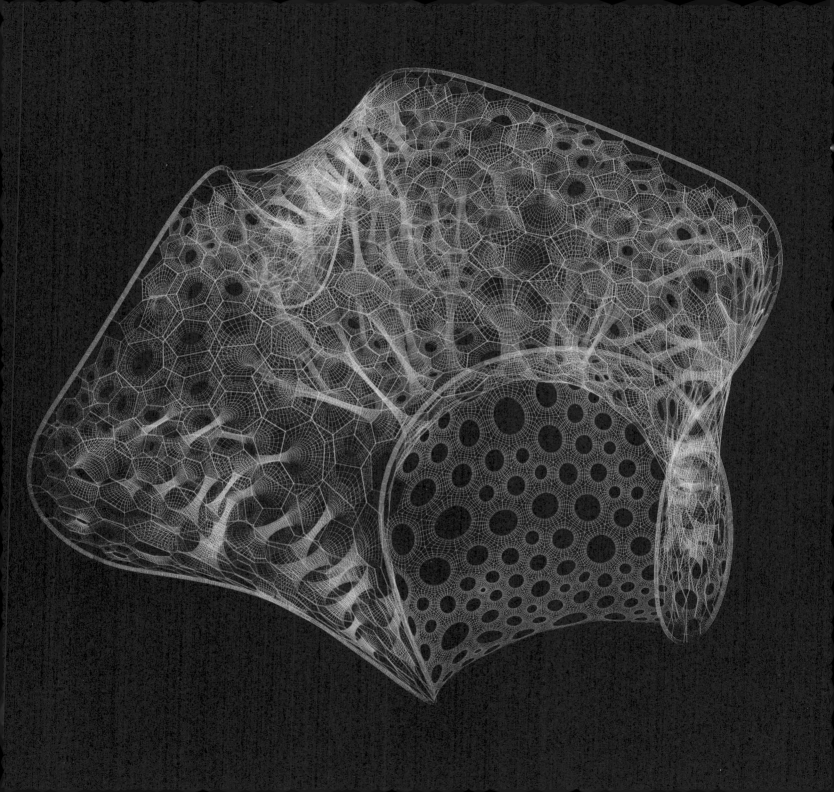

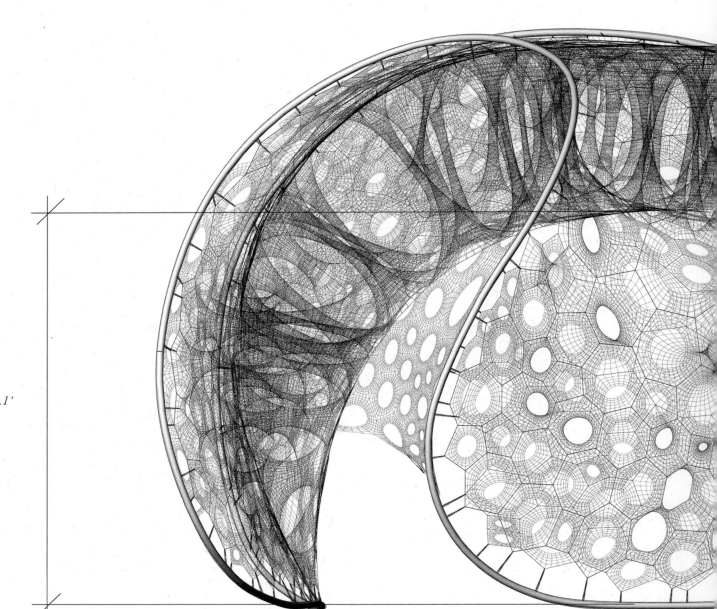

7.1'

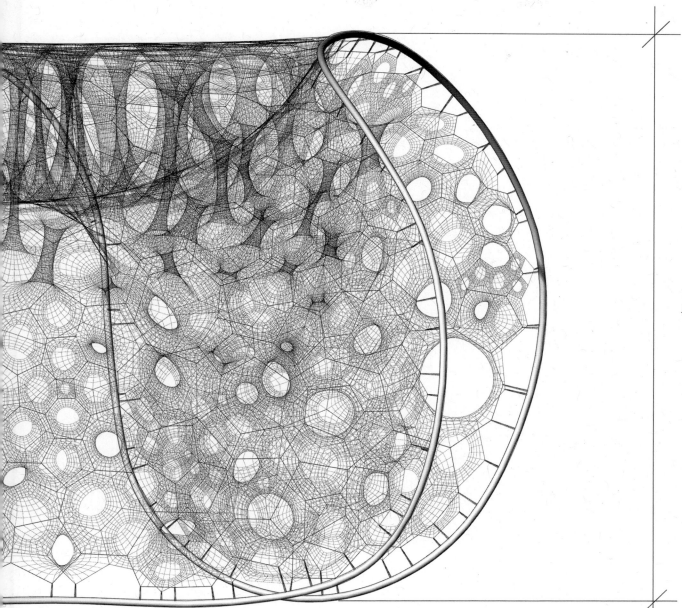

10.4'

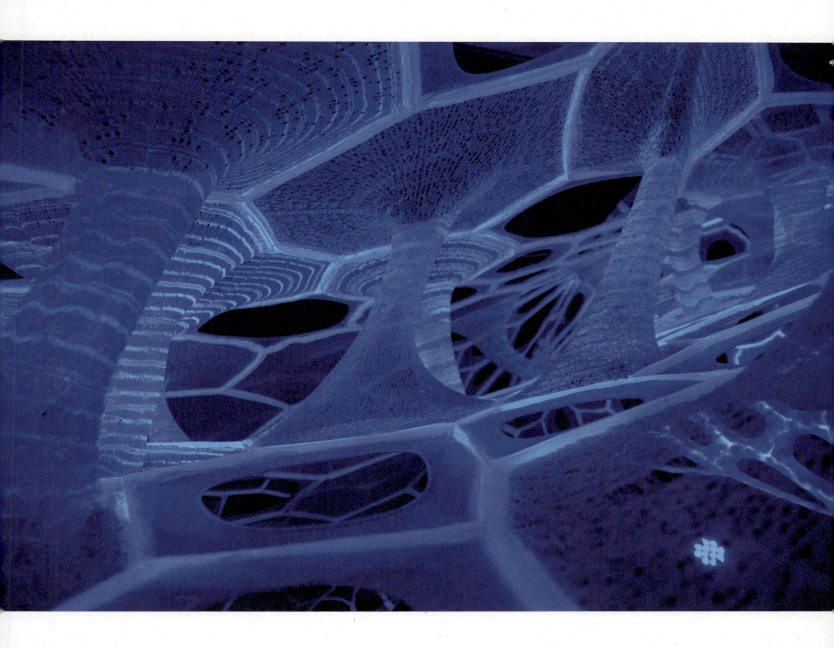

This research explores the intersection of digital ceramics and additive manufacturing through the projects PolyBrick and PolyTile, focussing on the customization of ceramic components for architecture using 3D printing. The aim is to achieve mass customization and intricate designs inspired by natural forms. As a demonstrator project and spatial prototype, PolyMorph (featured right) by JSS further advanced the techniques and concepts of digital ceramics. PolyBrick 1.0 introduced algorithmic design for nonstandard ceramic bricks, using wood joinery techniques for mortarless assembly. PolyBrick 2.0 applied principles from bone formation to create adaptive, porous brick structures, enhancing structural integrity and material expression through robotic 3D printing. PolyBrick 3.0 integrates DNA-steered materials, featuring bioengineered hydrogel for advanced functionality and environmental responsiveness. These innovations aim to pioneer adaptive architecture using additive manufacturing and biologically informed design processes, expanding the possibilities for sustainable building materials and interactive architectural surfaces. The work includes advances in digital technology, advanced geometry and material practices in arts, crafts and design disciplines. Leveraging the complex geometries inherently available in 3D printing, we can embed multiple layers of data simultaneously, creating forms that can respond locally to globally relevant conditions such as structural loading, spatial context and geometric orientation. The fabrication process across the phases of the PolyBrick series demonstrates a very high level of material efficiency, generating minimal waste and requiring no additional materials for the aggregation of parts. Through a controlled, mass-customized approach that seamlessly integrates design and production, the incorporation of ceramic bricks and modules in architecture is now within reach. JSLab at Cornell University has effectively designed a series of strategies for 3D printing ceramic brick assemblies at various scales and in DNA steered materials.

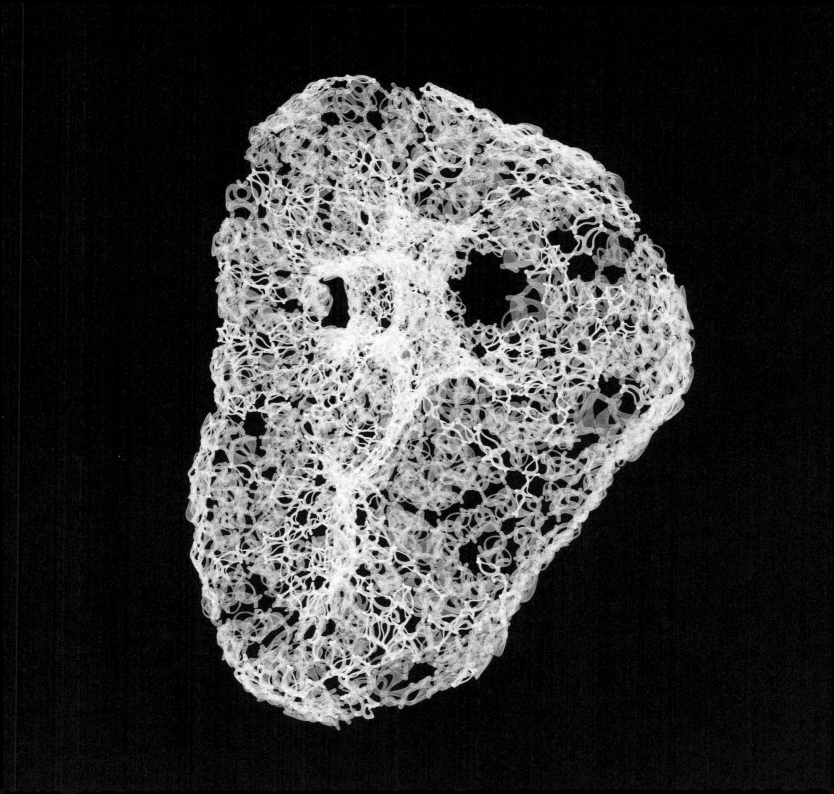

PolyBrick 1.0

This first series employs algorithmic design techniques for the digital fabrication and production of nonstandard ceramic brick components, for the mortarless assembly and installation of 3D printed, fired ceramic bricks. Seeking to achieve a system that required no additional adhesives or mortar, JSLab looked to traditional wood joinery techniques, developing a customized tapered dovetail. The tapering joint direction and angle are dependent upon the local geometric orientation of each component, allowing for precise interlocking of adjacent bricks.

PolyBrick 2.0

This series is generated with the rules, principles and behaviour of bone formation. In collaboration with Dr. Christopher Hernandez, an expert in the biomechanics of bone, the project focusses on the highly adaptive nature of bone to habitual loading, particularly present within the cancellous trabecular core of the bone. This heterogeneous lattice structure undergoes cyclic regeneration in response to repeated loading scenarios. Bio-inspired methods based on directional load adaptation have led to innovations in toolpath design for robotic 3D printing of complex porous geometries such as adaptive re-thickening through feedback between the digital model and the printed result. These analogue bone-informed methods produce variegated bricks that are light and porous at the top of a wall and dense at the base to carry load and maintain efficient structural integrity.

PolyBrick 3.0

JSLab explores the possibilities of living surface architecture through the integration of DNA-steered materials. In collaboration with the Dan Luo Lab at Cornell University, the project explores programmable bio-functionalities in our constructed architectural environments through the development of advanced ceramic bio-tiles. Synthetically designed with advanced bioengineering, this research uses DNA to design with light where unique signatures fluoresce within the PolyBrick clay body. The DNA stamps within the PolyBricks can store environmental information and use fluorescence to communicate back that data to impact both the local environment and inform humans of conditions within their local contexts.

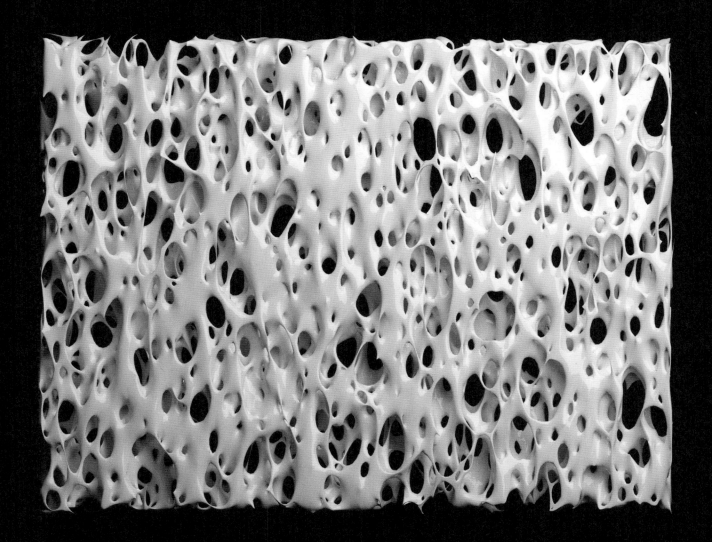

PolyBrick 3.0

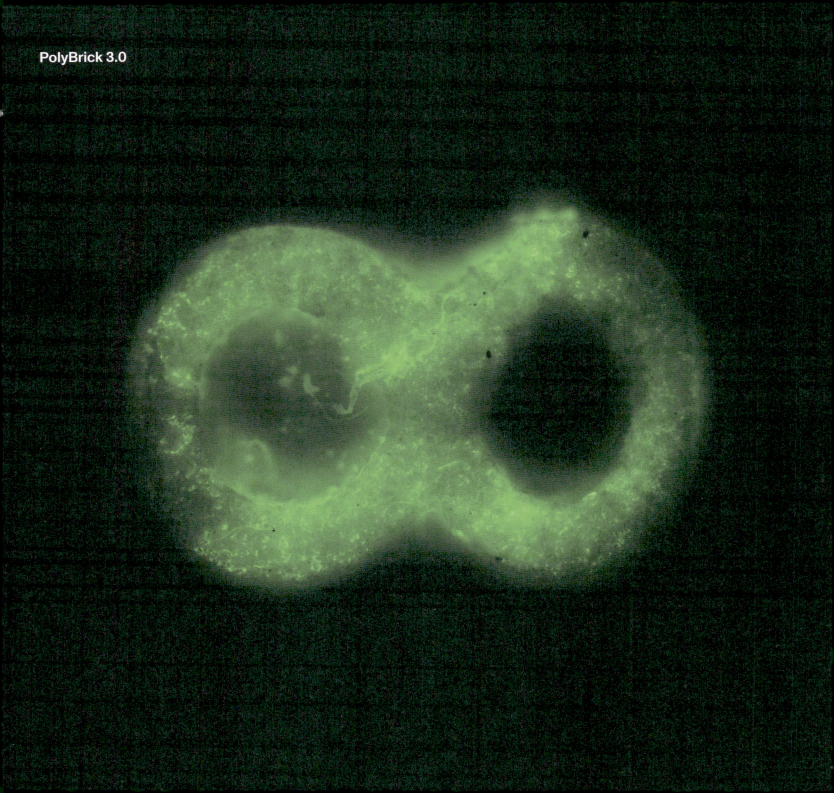

Morphogenesis shapes and differentiates cells, tissues and organs in biological systems through iterative multicellular network interactions with the environment. JSLab's work demonstrates how design-driven philosophies from 3D spatial biology, materials science, engineering and architecture can lead to significant advances in both scientific research, design processes and architectural practice. By exploring dynamic feedback loops between environment and biological form, this approach fosters a design philosophy rooted in biological concepts of emergence, robustness and morphogenesis. This interdisciplinary method integrates biology, engineering and architecture, promoting a biosynthetic design process where analogue results manifest as surface architecture responsive to environmental and internal programmed systems. The research focusses on evolving material and digital complexity in the built environment through prototypical design experiments that abstract and translate dynamic biological behaviors. The design process fluidly combines analog and digital techniques, incorporating human or digital handcraft to negotiate scale and complex behaviours.

This project aims to take shape design to the next level such that architecture is able to function in changing environmental conditions. Likewise, the ability of complex biological systems to thrive in changing environmental conditions depends on their ability to adapt, altering their form and function. During development in both animals and plants, cells must grow, specialize and form the complex shapes of organs. In plants, tissues can be induced to form unorganized cell masses that regenerate into new organisms as a form of biodiversity conservation. In brain cancer, tumours generate new tissue forms, which then compete with surrounding tissue for growth. The project tests the core hypothesis – that all of these diverse biological systems use a parallel emergent network connecting the system with the environment, a rule of life, to achieve their shapes – and that this same emergent network can be applied to architectural design to generate adaptable, robust and resilient structures.

This markedly contrasts with the prevailing dogma that biological and architectural morphogenesis is controlled via a forward genetic programme, without iterative feedback from the biophysical environment. Each step of the cyclical emergence network is tested through three experimental techniques in evolving biophysical environments applied to four diverse biological systems: chick hearts, *Arabidopsis* flowers (featured right), brain cancer in mice and regenerating *Arabidopsis* somatic embryos. These morphogenetic design rules are modelled and employed to create a robust bio-inspired, load-bearing facade system with emergent properties. This structure will mediate between fluctuating interior and exterior climatic conditions, including light, temperature, humidity and airflow in response to an ever-evolving environment. How robust, resilient and adaptable forms emerge over multiple cycles of this emergent multicellular network are explored.

Building upon JSLab's ongoing work, the PolyMorph project by Jenny Sabin Studio for The Frac Centre-Val de Loire explored morphogenesis and biological networks and fabricated material assemblies to address novel applications of non-standard ceramic components towards the production of 3D-textured prototypes and systems.

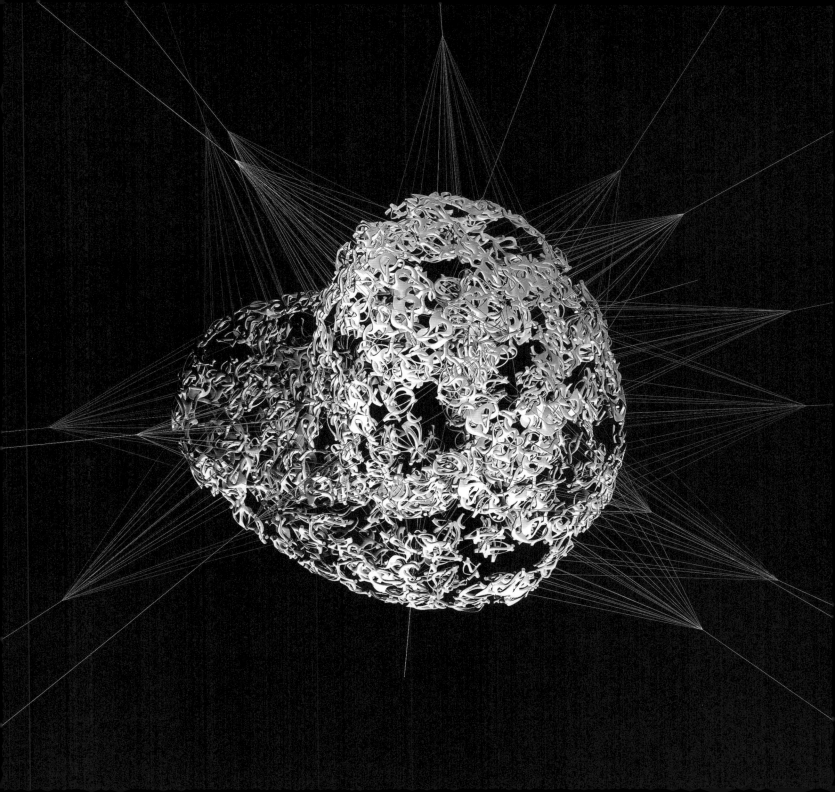

The dynamic reciprocity between environment and form explored through collaborative research on morphogenesis in the JSLab, informs analogue design processes and active feedback mechanisms in every JSS project. Named after the physical phenomena of waves undulating across the grasslands, Eddy features a data-driven lighting system steered in real-time by wind data gathered from the local environment. The project is inspired by the Grassland biome that also informed the collaborative design by BIG and Heatherwick Studio for the Bay View Building. Grasses and shrubs typically dominate these areas, but occasional robust trees survive having adapted to harsh climates with characteristics such as fire-resistant bark. Like the trees, Eddy and Shroud emanate a sense of quality of place and experience.

Fabric components at the base of the structure feature the densest array of cones with the gradient decreasing towards the upper regions of the project. The structure for Eddy is arranged in the shape of a hyperboloid of one sheet. It is bounded on the top by a tubular steel ring and at the base by a four-legged tubular steel arch. The arch is stiffened at its base by four tubular braces that branch off the main arch. The surface of the hyperboloid is structured as a diagrid with eight primary tubular steel elements forming the primary diagrid and 24 solid rod elements forming a secondary diagrid. The diagrid is spanned by power stretch fabric elements with colourful cone inserts that fill in the apertures in the diagrid to give the surface both a perforated and solid appearance. The fabric elements are extremely light and require minimal pre-stress to hold their shape. The structure is designed such that the primary tubular steel diagrid, arches and top ring can support the gravity and seismic demands on the entire structure.

Sharing material and formal strategies with Eddy, Shroud features a custom double membrane fabric structure tensioned within a connected series of undulating curved steel hoops that together envelop the stair.

Integrated with their context as two unique architectural elements, an important aim of Eddy and Shroud was to compliment and be in dialogue with the multitiered canopy system of the Bay View Building.

Client
Google Inc.

Location
Google Bay View Campus, Mountain View, CA, USA

Year
2022

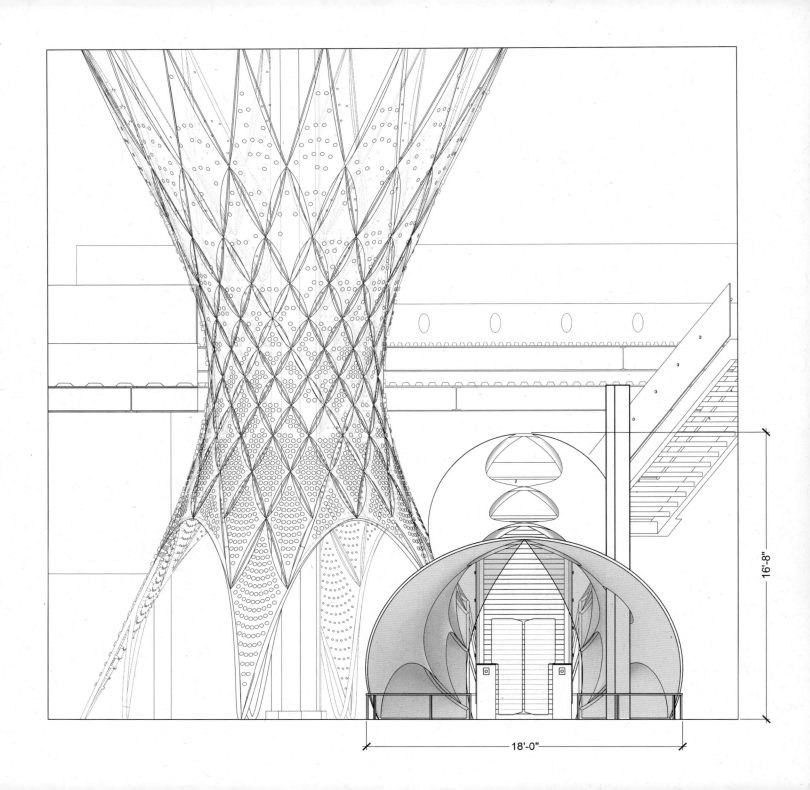

16'-8"

18'-0"

Colour changes and the engagement with light across scales are central to nearly all of Jenny Sabin Studio's projects, rooted in the foundational work of the Sabin+Jones LabStudio and their eSkin project with materials scientist Shu Yang. eSkin explored responsive materials and sensors from nano to macro scales, aiming to understand and manipulate material features like colour, transparency and opacity through changes in pattern, geometry and structure. This process generates structural colour – colour created by optical effects like refraction or interference, rather than pigment – resulting in hues that vary with the viewer's angle. Inspired by natural examples like the Blue Morpho butterfly and hummingbird feathers, Sabin's work translates these effects into scalable building skins, glazing and materials. Imagine dynamically blocking sunlight through simple mechanical changes in responsive film stretched or compressed to generate your own window. This research has been applied in projects like ColorFolds by JSLab, and ChromaFold and PolyForm by Jenny Sabin Studio.

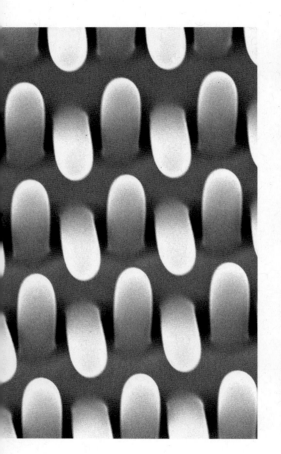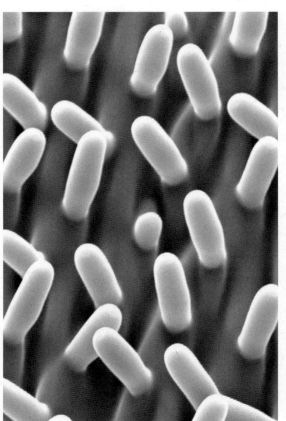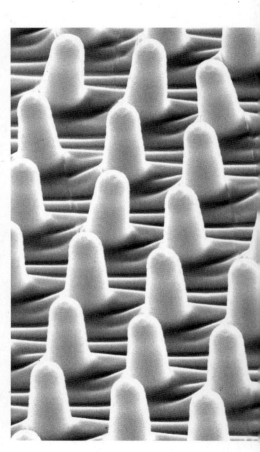

This project innovates the design and engineering of building-integrated solar cells by using computer design and 3D printing to create site-specific solar collection systems with customized filters and panels. Drawing on biological adaptations, including how sunflowers move after the sun and lithops plants filter light, Jenny Sabin Lab in collaboration with Mariana Bertoni and the DEfECT Lab at Arizona State University explore new configurations of solar panels that are both aesthetically pleasing and maximize energy conversion efficiency. This 1:1 scale prototype demonstrates a building-integrated photovoltaic system with extremely low greenhouse gas emissions, showcasing the potential of bio-inspired sustainable design.

Well-integrated and properly designed photovoltaics can play a pivotal role in increasing the use of renewable energy in architectural design. This research introduces alternative workflows and algorithms for manufacturing highly customized photovoltaic cells with integration of unique design features. Through advancements in computational design, simulation and 3D printing, this project explores the integration of spatial experience, aesthetics and efficiency into the architectural design process of photovoltaics. The exposed face of lithops plants receives high irradiance. As such, it contains filter mechanisms and a dispersed cellular arrangement to allow for cooling. Inspired by this structure, the design consists of three levels: a photovoltaic cell layer for solar generation, a dichroic grid shell for light filtration and a structural HDPE frame. The dichroic laminated panels diffuse light and create dynamic enhancing atmospheric effects, captivating the phenomena and performance of light absorption for energy generation. The result is a set of algorithms and workflows that provide architects and engineers with a design process that integrates customizable photovoltaic assemblies into sustainable architecture and aesthetics.

Client
Cornell University College of Human Ecology

Location
Ithaca, New York, USA

Year
2015-2021

PolyForm engages personalized architecture through design science at the Center of Human Ecology. By bridging the nano scale to the human scale through advancements in digital fabrication and emerging materials, this project promotes communication and active exchange across disciplines. PolyForm is a permanent public installation of four perforated, crystalline metal forms framing a high-trafficked thoroughfare on the Cornell University Campus. Building upon JSLab's ongoing collaborative work on structural color and through advancements in computational design and contemporary digital fabrication techniques, the project generates a responsive and ornamented architectural intervention that envelopes and activates daily routines and exchanges at Cornell's College of Human Ecology (CHE). PolyForm is not a literal translation of human ecology but embodies its themes through a dynamic interplay of light, colour and shadow that works across scales. The generative design process included the development of algorithms and topological modelling strategies to procedurally explore subdivision, folding and fractal growth.

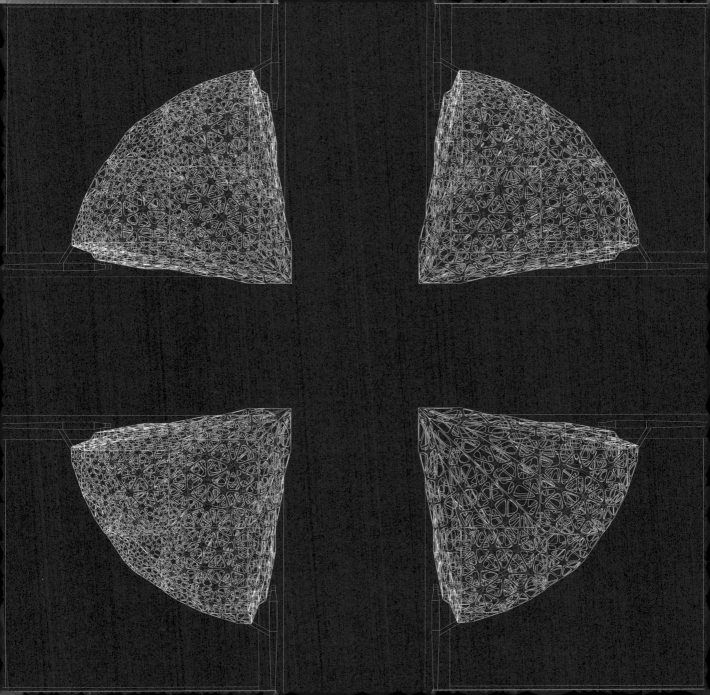

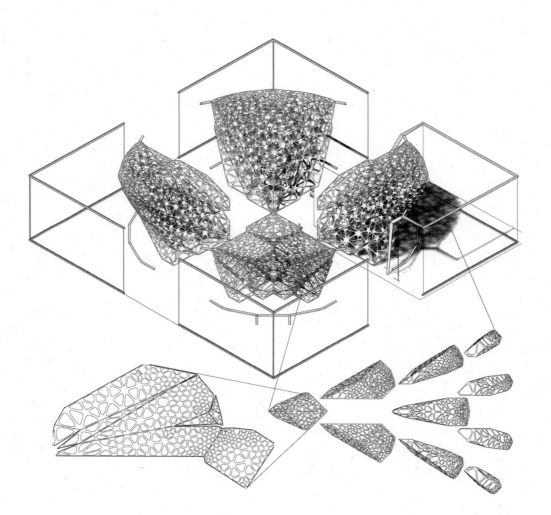

JSLab is pioneering the development of adaptive and responsive materials that exhibit structural colour changes, exploring the potential to enhance these effects through kirigami geometry – a technique involving folding combined with strategic cuts and holes. The lab's innovative approach includes the design of kirigami patterns through mesh optimization and the integration of cut and fold patterns. Research focusses on dual composite kirigami materials and actuated materials, such as shrinky dink films, shape memory alloys and shape memory polymers.

Kirigami, like origami (with "kiru" meaning "to cut" in Japanese, and "gami" meaning "paper"), brings new techniques, algorithms and processes to the creation of open, deployable and adaptive structural elements and architectural surfaces. JSLab's kirigami models incorporate geometric and biomimetic principles to design materials that adapt to external stimuli, such as heat, light and human interaction. By synthesizing design, material properties and kirigami programming, the lab achieves complex emergent behaviors from simple actions. Recent advancements move away from mechanical systems, focussing on integrated panel-and-hinge assemblies with 3D printed, programmable geometries and materials that respond elastically to stimuli.

Projects like ColorFolds and PolyForm illustrate how geometric variation within foldable assemblies can produce structural colour changes based on the participant's position, the surface's geometry and the lighting conditions.

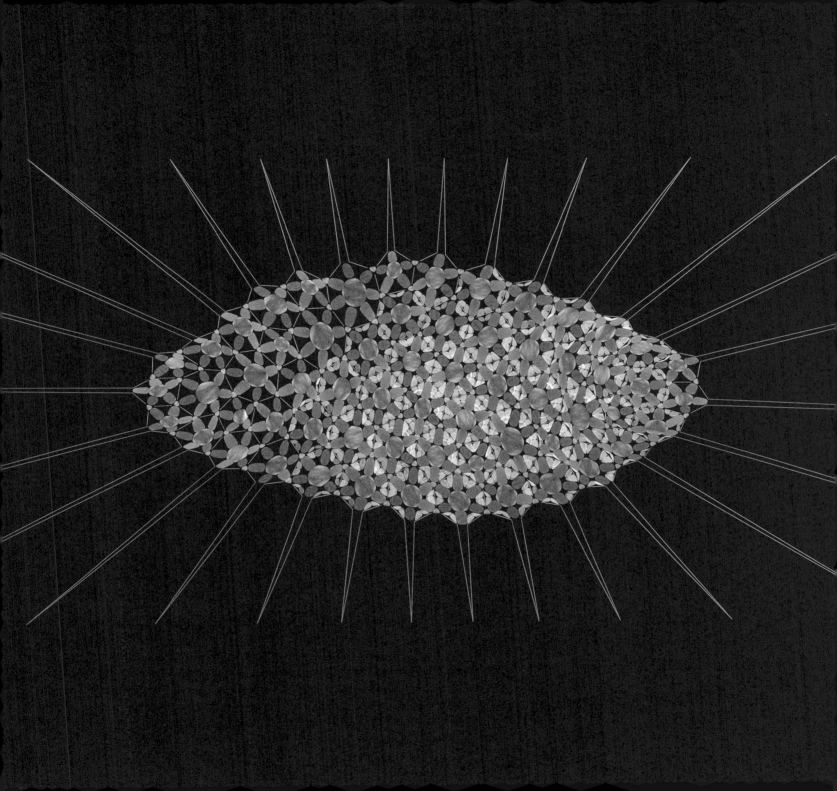

ColorFolds
ColorFolds combines novel surface materials with nitinol linear actu-
ators to create responsive environments. It uses customized digital
tools and algorithms to generate deployable geometries and architectural surfaces that adapt to complex curvature, with higher component densities in tighter areas. Each component features dichroic
film, a colour-changing material. Sensors detect the presence of
people, triggering Flexinol® spring systems that open or close the
folded components.

Location
Cornell Council for the Arts, Ithaca, New York, USA

Year
2015

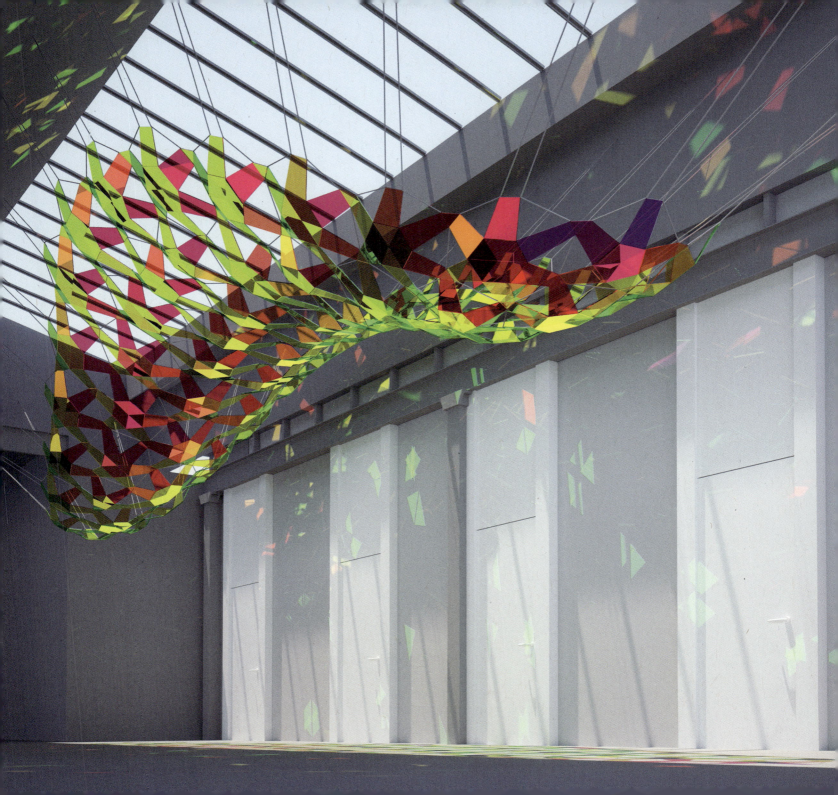

Client
Ontario Science Center

Location
Toronto, Canada

Year
2022-2023

ChromaFold
ChromaFold incorporates principles of structural colour and transparency at the human scale. This project, displayed at the Ontario Science Center, features a tessellated array of components that fold and unfold in response to people's movements. It uses a gradient of dichroic film and soft, translucent rice paper to interact with light, creating dynamic visual effects as the components are actuated by a system of sensors, spring systems, Arduino boards and motors.

nology. His award-winning *Architecture in the Age of Printing* (MIT Press, 2001) has been translated into several languages. His most recent books are *The Alphabet and the Algorithm* (2011); *The Second Digital Turn: Design Beyond Intelligence* (2017); and *Beyond Digital. Design and Automation at the End of Modernity* (2023), all published by the MIT Press.

Jan Boelen is a curator of design, architecture and contemporary art. Artistic director and co-founder of Atelier LUMA, a bioregional design lab in Arles, France since 2016. In 2001 Boelen founded Z33 House for contemporary art in Hasselt, Belgium and acted as Artistic Director till 2019. Founder of the Master Social design at the Design Academy of Eindhoven till 2020 and Rector of the Karlsruhe University of Arts and Design 2019-2023. In 2014 he curated BIO50, the design biennial of Ljubljana in Slovenia. He was Curator of the 4th Istanbul Design Biennial (2018) and initiated Manifesta 9 in Belgium (2012). Lastly, Boelen curated the Lithuanian Pavilion *Planet of People* in the Venice Architecture Biennial (2021).

Mario Carpo is Reyner Banham Professor of Architectural Theory and History, the Bartlett School of Architecture, UCL London. His research and publications focus on the history of early modern architecture and on the theory and criticism of contemporary design and tech-

Mette Marie Kallehauge is a curator at Louisiana Museum of Modern Art. In addition to *Living Structures*, she has most recently curated the exhibition series *The Architect's Studio*.

Claudia Pasquero is an architect, curator, author and educator; her work and research operates at the intersection of biology, computation and design. She is co-founder of ecoLogicStudio in London, Professor of Landscape Architecture, founder of the Synthetic Landscape Lab and Head of Institute for IOUD at Innsbruck University, Associated Professor and Director of the Urban Morphogenesis Lab at the Bartlett UCL in London. Head Curator of the Tallinn Architecture Biennale 2017, co-author of *The World Dubai Marine Life Incubator: Eco Machines V.3.0* (2010); *Systemic Architecture: Operating Manual for the Self-Organizing City* (2012); *Biodesign in the Age of Artificial Intelligence: Deep Green* (2023).

Marco Poletto is an architect, educator and innovator based in London. He is co-founder and Director of eco-LogicStudio and the design innovation venture Photo-Synthetica. He holds a PhD from RMIT University, Melbourne, and has been Unit Master at the Architectural Association in London, Visiting Critic at Cornell University and Research Cluster leader at The Bartlett, UCL. He currently lectures at the University of Innsbruck and the IAAC in Barcelona. Co-author of *The World Dubai Marine Life Incubator: Eco Machines V.3.0* (2010); *Systemic Architecture: Operating Manual for the Self-Organizing City* (2012); *Biodesign in the Age of Artificial Intelligence: Deep Green* (2023).

Jenny E. Sabin is the Arthur L. and Isabel B. Wiesenberger Professor in Architecture and the inaugural Chair for the Department of Design Tech at the Cornell College of Architecture, Art and Planning where she co-established a new advanced research degree in Design Technology. She is Principal of Jenny Sabin Studio, an experimental architectural design studio based in Ithaca and Director of the JSLab at Cornell AAP. Her book, *LabStudio: Design Research Between Architecture and Biology*, co-authored with Peter Lloyd Jones, was published in July 2017. In that same year, Sabin won MoMA & MoMA PS1's Young Architects Program with her submission, *Lumen*.

Hashim Sarkis is Dean of the MIT School of Architecture and Planning. Prior to that he was the Aga Khan Professor of Landscape Architecture and Urbanism at Harvard University Graduate School of Design. He has held numerous visiting appointments around the world including the American University of Beirut and the Metropolis Program in Barcelona. In addition to his academic work, Hashim Sarkis is Principal Architect in the Cambridge and Beirut based firm, HashimSarkis Studios, founded in 1998. His architectural and planning projects include affordable housing, institutional buildings and town planning throughout the globe.

Mette Ramsgaard Thomsen is Professor at the Royal Danish Academy – Architecture, Design, Conservation. She examines the intersection of architecture and computational design and founded the Centre for Information Technology and Architecture (CITA) in 2005, pioneering research into digital-material relations. Her interests in sustainability and bio-based materials have led to a focus on reparatory practice and systems of return. Her leadership extends to global platforms; she is the Paul Philippe Cret Visiting Professor at University of Pennsylvania and served as General Reporter for the 2023 UIA World Congress of Architects, advocating for sustainable architecture aligned with UN SDGs.

ecoLogicStudio

Deep Forest, p. 22
Project by: ecoLogicStudio (Prof Claudia Pasquero, Dr Marco Poletto)
Academic partners: Innsbruck University, The Bartlett UCL.
Project team: Prof Claudia Pasquero, Dr Marco Poletto with Jasper Zehetgruber, Beyza Nur Armağan, Konstantina Bikou, Xiao Wang, Alessandra Poletto
Prototyping support team: Jonas Wohlgenannt, Korbinian Enzinger, Felix Humml, Bo Liu, Mika Schulz, Michael Unterberger, Francesca Turi, Marco Matteraglia

GAN-Physarium: La Dérive Numérique, p. 30
Artist: ecoLogicStudio (Claudia Pasquero, Marco Poletto)
Academic partners: Synthetic Landscape Lab at Innsbruck University, Urban Morphogenesis Lab at the Bartlett UCL
Project Team Biopainting: Claudia Pasquero, Marco Poletto with Greta Ballschuh, Sheng Cao, Alessandra Poletto
Project team AI video: Claudia Pasquero, Marco Poletto with Joy Boulois, Korbinian Enzinger, Oscar Villarreal

TreeOne, p. 36
TreeOne, 2023, robotically 3D printed algal biopolymers, lab grade borosilicate glass, living cultures of Cyanidium Caldarium in liquid medium, 670 × 1.350 × 620 cm
Project by ecoLogicStudio (Claudia Pasquero, Marco Poletto)
Project team: Claudia Pasquero, Marco Poletto with Kostantina Bikou, Haoyi Chen, Seung Joon Oh, Alessandra Poletto, Emiliano Rando, Engjell Rodiqi, Xiao Wang
Academic partners: The Synthetic Landscape Lab at Innsbruck University, The Urban Morphogenesis Lab at the Bartlett UCL.
Prototyping support: Beijing Dileyou, Nagami, Synthetic Landscape Lab

AirBubble, p. 44
Project name: AirBubble – A project by ecoLogiStudio for Otrivin Breathe Clean
Architect: ecoLogicStudio (Claudia Pasquero, Marco Poletto)
Project team: Claudia Pasquero, Marco Poletto with Eirini Tsomokou,

Korbinian Enzinger, Riccardo Mangili, Georgios Drakontaeidis, Alessandra Poletto, Terezia Greskova
Academic partners: Synthetic Landscape Lab IOUD Innsbruck University, Urban Morphogenesis Lab BPRO The Bartlett UCL

BioBombola, p. 50
Architect: ecoLogicStudio (Claudia Pasquero, Marco Poletto)
Project team: Claudia Pasquero, Marco Poletto with Georgios Drakontaeidis, Riccardo Mangili, Eirini Tsomokou
BioBombola is part of Photo.Synth.Etica www.photosynthetica.co.uk, an ongoing research programme, started in 2018 and developed by ecoLogicStudio in partnership with the Urban Morphogenesis Lab BPRO of The Bartlett UCL and the Synthetic Landscape Lab of the University of Innsbruck

H.O.R.T.U.S. XL Astaxathin.g, p. 54
H.O.R.T.U.S. XL Astaxanthin.g, 2019, 3D printed substratum, micro-algae in biogel medium, 320 × 272 × 114 cm
Design: ecoLogicStudio (Claudia Pasquero, Marco Poletto)
Project team: Konstantinos Alexopoulos, Matteo Baldissarra, Michael Brewster
Academic Partners: Synthetic Landscape Lab, IOUD, Innsbruck University (Prof. Claudia Pasquero, Maria Kuptsova, Terezia Greskova, Emiliano Rando, Jens Burkart, Niko Jabadari, Simon Posch); Photosynthetica consortium (www.photosynthetica.co.uk); CREATE Group / WASP Hub Denmark – University of Southern Denmark (SDU) (Prof. Roberto Naboni, Furio Magaraggia); Urban Morphogenesis Lab BPRO The Bartlett UCL
Structural engineering: YIP structural engineering

Photo.Synth.Etica, p. 58
Architect: ecoLogicStudio (Claudia Pasquero and Marco Poletto)
Design team: Konstantinos Alexopoulos, Nico Aulitzky, Shlok Soni, Robert Staples, Chrysi Vrantsi, Chia Wei Yang
Structural Engineering: YIP structural engineering

Synthetic Landscape Lab: Landscapes of Biodegradability Project, p. 60
The first installation of these biodegradable sculptures in the Alpine landscape at Universitätszentrum Obergurgl took place in May 2023, forming a striking land art project. The project explores how the biodegradation process can contribute to the biodiversity of the Alpine microbiomes, nurturing the landscape and fostering ecological remediation.
Faculty: Prof Claudia Pasquero, Dr Marco Poletto, Korbinian Enzinger, Emiliano Rando, Terezia Greskova, Xiao Wang, Maria Kusptsova, Haoyi Chen, Vadim Samthkin, Boh Liu, Sheng Meng. Students: Franz Adler,

Zech Julia, Maximilian Mayrl, Paula Malcher, Lynn Federspiel, Michael Unterberger, Beyza Armagan, Yannik Piejede, Jhonas Wohlgenent, Marco Frauser, Martina Stoppel, Felix Dallago, Lorena Schrott, Viviane Lau, Jan Schambach, Elisa Dolenz, Götsch Kilian, Lorenzo Sitzia, Katharina Cacioli, Rostislav Popov, Aleksandra Panina, EcoSki, Selina Janssen, Paulin Ruhrmann, Alessio Trucios, Lia Patscheider, Ferstl Hanna, Humml Felix, Jochen Kateryna
The Synthetic Landscape Lab is conducting a research project titled "Landscapes of Biodegradability". The Synthetic Landscape Lab was founded in 2017 at the University of Innsbruck, in collaboration with ecoLogicStudio

XenoDerma, p. 66
XenoDerma, 2018, spider silk morphologies (Asian Fawn Tarantulas) informed by 3D printed substratum, 118 × 34 × 93 cm
ecoLogicStudio archive (Claudia Pasquero, Marco Poletto)
Design, Production and Research: Urban Morphogenesis Lab (Lab Director: Prof. Claudia Pasquero; Cluster Researchers: Filippo Nassetti, Emmanouil Zaroukas; Design Team: Mengxuan Lii, Xiao Liang); Urban Morphogenesis Lab BPRO The Bartlett UCL

Atelier LUMA

Magasin électrique, p. 77
LUMA Arles – Atelier LUMA
Assemble
BC ARCHITECTS & STUDIES
BC MATERIALS

Salt, p. 88
Compagnie des Salins du Midi et salines de l'Est
Henna Burney (Atelier LUMA)
Alexandre Echasseriau
Karlijn Sibbel

Sunflowers, p. 96
LCA – ENSIACET
Henna Burney (Atelier LUMA)
Tiago Almeida (Atelier LUMA)
Carlotta Borgato (Atelier LUMA)

Humlebæk biopolymer switches, p. 100
Authentic Material
LCA – ENSIACET
DanskTang

Seed center Humlebaek
Henna Burney (Atelier LUMA)
Anne-Claire Hostequin (Atelier LUMA)

Bioplastics, p. 106
Anne-Claire Hostequin (Atelier LUMA)
Jordi Cansouline (Atelier LUMA)
Studio Klarenbeek&Dros
Roto 30
Vegeplast
DanskTang
Seed center Humlebaek

Unwanted species, p. 112
Fritz Hansen Team
Laboratoire AMVALOR, école des Arts et Métiers de Cluny
Arnaud Magnin (Atelier LUMA)
Jordi Cansouline (Atelier LUMA)
Axelle Gisserot (Atelier LUMA)
Anne-Claire Hostequin (Atelier LUMA)
Marie Marquet

Dyed fabrics, p. 116
Chromologics
Axelle Gisserot (Atelier LUMA)
Mathilde Laroche (Atelier LUMA)
Marie Marquet (Atelier LUMA)
Antonio Navarro (Atelier LUMA)
Adèle Nicoleau (Atelier LUMA)

Local layer, p. 122
Anne Claire Hostequin (Atelier LUMA)
Carlotta Borgato (Atelier LUMA)
Jordi Cansouline (Atelier LUMA)
Anna Perugini

Cartographies, p. 126
Clara Kernreuter
Paul Vachon
Studio SOC (Société des Objets Cartographiques)

Exhibition coordination
Lucie Colleu
Editorial coordination
Marie Pradayrol

Jenny Sabin Studio

Lumen, p. 140
Design Team
A project by Jenny Sabin Studio, 2017
Principal and Lead Architectural Designer: Jenny E. Sabin
Project Lead and Manager: Dillon Pranger
Design and Production: Jordan Berta (Content Coordination),
Diego Garcia Blanco, Elie Boutros, Daniel Villegas Cruz, Omar Dairi,
Alejandro Garcia, Andres Gutierrez, Jingyang Liu Leo (senior research
associate), Mark Lien, Jasmine Liu, Andrew Moorman, Christopher
Morse, Bennett Norman, Marwan Omar, Sasson Rafailov, Steve Ren,
David Rosenwasser, Danny Salamoun (production lead),
Aishwarya Sreenivas, Raksarat Vorasucha
Engineering Design: Clayton Binkley & Kristen Strobel, Arup
Fabricators and Installers: Tom Carruthers, Bo Jacobsson, Erik Grinde,
Spencer Whynaucht, Todd Fitcher, Ryan Fitcher, Shannon McElree,
Mateo Baca, Jacobsson Carruthers, LLC
Knit Fabrication: Tom Shintaku, Shima Seiki WHOLEGARMENT
Lighting Design: Juan Pablo Lira and Hilary Manners, Focus Lighting
Video: Cole Skaggs
Photography: Pablo Enriquez, Jesse Winter, Yuriy Chernets

PolyThread, p. 146
Design Team
A Project by Jenny Sabin Studio, 2016
Commissioned by Cooper Hewitt Smithsonian Design Museum for
"Beauty-Cooper Hewitt Design Triennial", 2016
Lead Architectural Designer: Jenny E. Sabin
Design and Production: Martin Miller, Charles Cupples
Engineering Designer: Arup
Knit Fabrication: Shima Seiki WHOLEGARMENT
Sewing and Finishing: Andrew Dahlgren and All Sewn Together

Digital Ceramics, p. 152
A research project by JSLab at Cornell University
PolyBrick 1.0
Jenny E. Sabin, Martin Miller, Nick Cassab, and Andrew Lucia
PolyBrick 2.0
Principal Investigators – Jenny E. Sabin & Christopher Hernandez
Team – Eda Begum Birol, Yao Lu, Colby Johnson, Ege Sekkin,
Cameron Nelson, David Moy, Yaseen Islam
PolyBrick 3.0
Principal Investigators – Jenny E. Sabin & Dan Luo
Team – David Rosenwasser, Shogo Hamada, Yehudah A. Pardo,

Kenneth G. Yancey
Scientific imagery provided by Dan Luo Group

PolyMorph, p. 153
A Project by Jenny Sabin Studio, 2013
Permanently installed at the FRAC Centre, Orléans, France and
originally featured in the 9th ArchiLab, *Naturalizing Architecture*
Architectural Designer and Artist: Jenny E. Sabin
Design and Production Team: Martin Miller, Jillian Blackwell,
Jin Tack Lim, Liangjie Wu, Lynda Brody
This project was funded jointly by Jenny Sabin Studio, the Pew
Fellowships in the Arts and the PCCW Affinito-Stewart Grant at
Cornell University

Understanding the Rules of Life: Emergent Networks, p. 162
The Understanding the Rules of Life: Emergent Networks project is
done in collaboration with principal investigator Adrienne Roeder
and funded by the National Science Foundation (NSF 4900,
Award # 2222434), 2021-current.
Principal Investigators: Adrienne Roeder (PI), Jenny Sabin,
Jonathan Butcher, David Odde, Marceline Egnin
Team: Julia Barnoin, Alba Ivania Rivera, Hung Ming Tseng, Byron
Rusnak, Xinlin Lu, Shuofei Sun, Steve Poon, Rohit Agarwal, Lanxi Hu
Scientific imagery provided by Roeder Lab and Butcher Lab
Branching Morphogenesis by Sabin+Jones LabStudio, 2008

Eddy and Shroud, p. 166
A Project by Jenny Sabin Studio, 2022
Principal and Lead Architectural Designer: Jenny E. Sabin
Project manager: Dillon Pranger
Design & Development: John Hilla, Claire Moriarty, Michael Paraszczak,
Hancheng Zhang
Engineering Design: Clayton Binkley, ODD Lot
Fabricators and Installers: One Hat One Hand
Sewing and Finishing: Rainier Industries Ltd.
Lighting Design: Jenny Sabin Studio
Photo Credits: Jenny Sabin Studio & One Hat One Hand

Structural Color Designing with Light, p. 170
The eSkin project is done in collaboration with principal investigator
Shu Yang and funded by the National Science Foundation Emerging
Frontiers in Research and Innovation, Science in Energy and
Environmental Design (NSF 7633, Award # 1038215), 2010-2014
Principal Investigators: Shu Yang (PI), Jenny Sabin, Nader Engheta,
Peter Lloyd Jones, and Jan van der Spiegel

Architecture Team: Andrew Lucia (Senior Personnel),
Simin Wang, Giffen Ott
Scientific imagery provided by Shu Yang Group

Sustainable Architecture and Aesthetics, p. 174
Sustainable Architecture and Aesthetics (SAA): Design and Engineering
for Customizable Photovoltaic Assemblies, 2018-2021
A research project by JSLab at Cornell University in collaboration with
the DEfECT Lab at Arizona State University
Principal Investigators: Jenny E. Sabin (PI) & Mariana Bertoni (Co-PI)
Research Team: Alexander Htet Kyaw, Anita Lin, Begum Birol,
Omar Dairi, Jeremy Bilotti, Allison Bernett, April Jeffries,
Mariana Bertoni, Jenny E. Sabin
Photography by Thanut Sakdanaraseth

This research project was generously funded by the National Academy
of Engineering Frontiers of Engineering Program and The Grainger
Foundation and administered by the National Academy of Sciences

PolyForm, p. 180
A project by Jenny Sabin Studio, 2015-2021
Principal and Lead Architectural Designer: Jenny E. Sabin
Project Manager: Dillon Pranger
Design & Production: Jordan Berta, Madeline Metawati Eggers,
Charles Cupples, John Hilla, Byungchan Ahn, Michael Paraszczak
Engineering Design: Clayton Binkley & Lucas Whitesell,
Arup Fabricators and Installers: Vance Fabrication, Accufab,
Pulp Studio, Inc.
Photo Credits: John Munson and Jason Koski

Folding Material Effects, p. 184
This research in collaboration with principal investigator Randall
Kamian is part of a second project funded by the National Science
Foundation in the JSLab at Cornell University: Kirigami in Architecture,
Technology, and Science (KATS) (NSF 12-583, Award # 1331583)
Principal Investigators: Randall Kamian (PI), Jenny Sabin,
Shu Yang, Dan Luo
ChromaFold by Jenny Sabin Studio, commissioned by the Ontario
Science Center, 2022-2023. Architectural Designer: Jenny E. Sabin
Design and Production: Claire Moriarty, Michael Paraszczak,
Haotian Ma, Kevin Guo
ColorFolds by JSLab, originally on view as part of the Cornell Council
for the Arts, 2015.
Architectural Designer: Jenny E. Sabin
Design and Production: Martin Miller, Daniel Cellucci, Andrew Moorman

Photo:
ecoLogicStudio
Photos and drawings: p. 23, 24 left, 25, 26, 27, 63, 64, 65 ©
SyntheticLandscapeLab; 24 right, 37, 38, 40, 41 © Arch-Exist; 28, 29, 32,
34, 35, 42, 43, 57 © ecoLogicStudio; 39 © Joonhwan Yoon; 45, 46, 47, 48,
49 © Maja Wirkus; 33, 51, 52, 53, 55, 56, 59, 60, 61 © NAARO; 31, 67, 68,
69 © Urban Morphogensis Lab The Bartlett UCL

Atelier LUMA
Photos © Adrian Deweerdt with the exception of: p. 81, 84 bottom, 107,
116, 117, 118, 119 © Joana Luz; p. 80, 85, 104, 123, 124 © Joseph Halligan;
p. 93 © Marc Domage; p. 92 © Henna Burney; p. 97 © Florent Gardin;
p. 109 top © Florian Tripoteau; p. 109 bottom © Henriette Waal; p. 113 ©
Arnaud Magnin; 121 © Emma Rigoulot. Mapping p. 127, 128, 128 © Atelier
LUMA & SOC Studio

Jenny Sabin Studio
Photos and scientific imagery: p. 141 © Yuriy Chernets; p. 143, 144, 145
© Pablo Enriquez; 150, 151, 155 © Cooper Hewitt Design Museum; 158,
159 © Dan Luo Lab and JSLab, Cornell University; 161 © Sabin+Jones
LabStudio, University of Pennsylvania; photo by Jenny Sabin; 163 ©
Adrienne Roeder Lab, Cornell University; 164, 167, 169, 189 © Jenny
Sabin Studio; 171, 176 bottom © Jenny Sabin; 172, 173 © Shu Yang Group,
University of Pennsylvania; 176 top, 177 © Thanut Sakdanaraseth; 183 ©
Jason Koski

Architecture Connecting
Living Structures
© 2024 Louisiana Museum of Modern Art, Lars Müller Publishers
and the contributors

Edited by Iben Engelhardt Andersen, Lærke Rydal Jørgensen
and Mette Marie Kallehauge
Graphic Design: Anni's
Translations: Adam King (Poul Erik Tøjner, Mette Marie Kallehauge
and Kjeld Kjeldsen) and Jane Rowley (Mette Marie Kallehauge)
Copy-editing: Sherilyn Nicolette Hellberg (conversations with
ecoLogicStudio and Jenny Sabin)
Proofreading: Henry Broome
Cover, front: PolyMorph by Jenny Sabin Studio, 2013. Permanently
installed at the FRAC Centre, Orléans, France and originally featured in
the 9th ArchiLab, Naturalizing Architecture. Drawing by Jenny Sabin
Mette Marie Kallehauge's text has been peer reviewed

Litho/Print: Narayana Press
ISBN Louisiana Museum of Modern Art: 978-87-93659-85-8
ISBN Lars Müller Publishers: 978-3-03778-780-9
Printed in Denmark 2024

Distributed in North America by ARTBOOK/D.A.P.
www.artbook.com

Louisiana Museum of Modern Art
Humlebæk, Denmark
www.louisiana.dk

Lars Müller Publishers
Zürich, Switzerland
www.lars-mueller-publishers.com

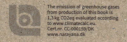

The emission of greenhouse gases
from production of this book is
1,3 kg CO2eq evaluated according
to www.climatecalc.eu.
Cert.nr. CC-000159/DK
www.narayana.dk

The catalogue is published on the occasion of the exhibition
Architecture Connecting
Living Structures
Louisiana Museum of Modern Art, Humlebæk
8 November 2024 – 23 March 2025

Curators: Mette Marie Kallehauge and Kjeld Kjeldsen
Curatorial Coordinator/Registrar: Marianne Ahrensberg
Exhibition Architects: Brian Lottenburger and Lovisa My Lorén
Conservator/Exhibition Producer: Jesper Lund Madsen
Graphic Design: Maria Hviid Bengtson, Marie Lübecker and
Thomas Joakim Winther
Intern: Thea Bakke-Olsen

Louisiana's architectural exhibitions are supported by Realdania
– a philanthropic association